CYBERSEX

CYBERSEX

The Dark Side of the Force

A Special Issue of the Journal *Sexual Addiction & Compulsivity*

Edited by
Al Cooper, Ph.D.

USA	Publishing Office:	BRUNNER-ROUTLEDGE
		A member of the Taylor & Francis Group
		325 Chestnut Street
		Philadelphia, PA 19106
		Tel: (215) 625-8900
		Fax: (215) 625-2940
	Distribution Center:	BRUNNER-ROUTLEDGE
		A member of the Taylor & Francis Group
		7625 Empire Drive
		Florence, KY 41042
		Tel: 1-800-634-7064
		Fax: 1-800-248-4724
UK		BRUNNER-ROUTLEDGE
		A member of the Taylor & Francis Group
		27 Church Road
		Hove
		E. Sussex, BN3 2FA
		Tel.: +44 (0) 1273 207411
		Fax: +44 (0) 1273 205612

CYBERSEX: THE DARK SIDE OF THE FORCE: A Special Issue of the Journal *Sexual Addiction & Compulsivity*

2 3 4 5 6 7 8 9 0

Printed by G. H. Buchanan, Philadelphia, PA, 2000.
Cover design by Rob Williams.

A CIP catalog record for this book is available from the British Library.
∞ The paper in this publication meets the requirements of the ANSI Standard Z39.48-1984 (Permanence of Paper).

Library of Congress Cataloging-in-Publication Data

Available upon request from the publisher.

ISBN 1-58391-305-X (paper)

CONTENTS

Preface

Cybersex and Sexual Compulsivity: The Dark Side of the Force

AL COOPER

When Pat Carnes and Jennifer Schneider asked me to guest edit this special edition of *Sexual Addiction & Compulsivity: The Journal of Treatment and Prevention*, I began to think about how to introduce this important collection of articles on the intersection of the Internet and computer technology, and sexual compulsion.

Most of us are not really aware that the Internet is profoundly changing every facet of our lives. The rate of growth for new Internet service is estimated to be a meteoric 25% every three months. Once separate technologies, telephones, televisions, and computers are merging—a phenomenon known as convergence. Work, school, and even social activities are increasingly dependent upon, and centered around, computers. Five years ago, most people could not even imagine the concept of online chatting or shopping. What unknowns lie ahead in the next five years? Even more striking is how quickly we adapt to and take for granted the technologies in our daily lives that were science fiction just an eyeblink ago.

This same phenomenon struck me while conducting a workshop in Israel this summer. Few places have such striking contrasts, such a confluence of the ancient and the new. Satellite dishes are inside the walls of Jerusalem. Cell phones are carried by Bedouins. The Internet is accessible on desktops and palm pilots throughout the land, carrying on it a new gospel of interconnectivity and (almost) instant communication. What better place to ponder whether the Information Age, through the medium of the Internet, will accelerate mankind's evolution along the path toward salvation, or toward demise.

Late one night while in Jerusalem, as I thought about this upcoming issue, it became clear to me that sexuality is similarly, and precariously, teetering on an ambiguous electronic precipice. Like the Bible, the Internet is filled with tales of the transforming power of romantic love, as well as the destructiveness of misguided sexuality. People are people and are beset

1

with yearnings, temptations, appetites, and lusts that have neither much changed, nor abated, over the millennia.

In that moment in the Eternal City, I realized that humans have always faced sexual choices with the potential to lead them to decadence or transcendence. However, unlike the days of the Old Testament, the added element of computer technology makes modern times qualitatively different. The "Triple A Engine" of Access, Affordability, and Anonymity combine to turbo-charge (i.e., accelerate and intensify) online sexual interactions. Flirtation and innuendo, long the staples of leisurely seduction, rapidly escalate into frank sexual discussions and proposals on the Internet. This abrupt and norm-changing shift evokes intense reactions. The speed, magnitude, and endless possibilities, as well as the attendant effects, are without precedent.

Lifestyle commentators are apt to categorize online sexual behaviors as "all good" or "all bad." Clearly, the Internet is a medium of communication and online sexuality is neither inherently good nor bad. Rather, it is the interaction of the content that the "purveyors" (those who host web sites, post to newsgroups, cruise chat rooms, etc.) offer and how "consumers" of these electronic gathering spots react and respond to these messages, images, and sounds that result in "good" or "bad" outcomes. I have written earlier about the numerous ways in which the Internet can positively impact sexuality, as well as have warned of the inherent dangers in online sexual pursuits.

This journal is devoted to a scholarly examination of the latter and the increasingly common clinical concerns of how sexual interactions on the Internet have the potential to exacerbate the problems of those already struggling to maintain some control of their sexual thoughts and behaviors. Similarly, there is the potential for vastly increasing the numbers of people to develop or compound distorted, constricted, and otherwise unhealthy associations with their sexuality as a result of their sexual surfing.

As with most new social phenomena, we are experiencing a lag in professional and theoretical discourse, most especially empirical investigations, that might shed some light on the myriad ways the Internet already does, and will continue to, influence sexuality. If those of us who work with sexual issues and relations are going to help others, we first need to have a better understanding of the powerful factors at play. That is the purpose of this special edition—to bring together some of the leaders in the field and provide them a forum on which to focus and elucidate the various dimensions of these issues.

The articles begin with a reanalysis of the largest study ever conducted on Internet sexuality by Cooper, Delmonico, and Burg. Their findings on cybersex compulsivity, populations at risk, and the resulting implications are something all clinicians should be aware of if the area is ultimately to be built upon an empirical foundation. This is followed by Schneider's article, which also reports important new data from a survey corroborating the devastating effects of cybersex involvement on the families and partners of those involved in these activities. In addition, she offers a model outlining the prerecovery stages that partners go through. Young, Griffin-Shelley, Cooper, O'Mara, and Buchanan take a different look at cyberaffairs and their impact on couples. They provide a framework for understanding how people may find themselves involved in these situations, as well as clinical interventions and practical steps useful in addressing the fallout from these problems in couples therapy. Freeman-Longo looks more specifically at the effect of Internet sexuality on children and teens. He provides a number of interesting suggestions for parents and educators on how best to deal with the inevitable fact that young people will encounter sexual materials when going online. Putnam and Maheu offer a helpful insight into why online sexual behaviors are so problematic and suggest ways that the Internet can actually be used to facilitate and enhance treatment. They also look at how ethical, legal, and regulatory aspects of behavioral telehealth impact the form that this treatment might take. Orzack and Ross use case examples to illustrate inpatient and intensive outpatient modalities, and report data revealing a significant improvement for those treated in their program. They emphasize the importance of integrating the two treatments as the majority of patients that enter short-term inpatient treatment will require additional outpatient therapy. In their thought-provoking article, Schwartz and Johnson suggest that the Internet is the newest version of the "tea room" or "sexual marketing place" and posit an explanation for why this venue is so attractive in our society. They offer clinical data used to construct four subtypes of cybersex abusers, as well as a range of treatment interventions. Finally, to assist clinicians in having a better sense of the resources available on Internet sexual problems, Sealy reviews a new book on this topic, and Katehakis and Weiss provide a comprehensive review of the various Internet sites of 12-step fellowships for recovering sex addicts and their families.

As we enter this new age, we have a great opportunity, as well as a duty as mental health professionals and modern-day healers, to educate ourselves and the public about the significance and power of the Internet. If we wish to encourage love, intimacy, connection, and respect, we can direct and guide people to sex-positive web sites, forums, and online communities. If our clients struggle with destructive, limiting, isolating, and unsatisfying sexual interactions, we can help them to identify and resist the temptations and easy gratifications found online.

I believe that this collection of articles will become a central reference and repository for those who share an interest in online sexuality. In addition, I hope it will serve as a catalyst for more thought and creativity in its readers, as well as serve as the impetus for even more writing and research in this new and largely uncharted territory.

Finally, thanks to Coralie Scherer and Rob Weiss for their editorial input, and to all involved for sharing their perspectives, working so hard on a tight deadline, and, in the end, making this special issue possible. A special note of gratitude to Jennifer Schneider, who went way above and beyond her role as associate editor in helping me in innumerable ways with this project.

Chapter 1

Cybersex Users, Abusers, and Compulsives: New Findings and Implications

AL COOPER

San Jose Marital and Sexuality Centre, Santa Clara, California, USA

DAVID L. DELMONICO

Duquesne University, Pittsburgh, Pennsylvania, USA

RON BURG

Stanford University, Stanford, California, USA

Literature regarding sexual use of the Internet has primarily focused on anecdotal data of clinical cases. This study empirically examines the characteristics and usage patterns of individuals who use the Internet for sexual purposes. The Kalichman Sexual Compulsivity Scale was the primary tool used to divide the sample (n = 9,265) into four groups: nonsexually compulsive (n = 7,738), moderately sexually compulsive (n = 1,007), sexually compulsive (n = 424), and cybersex compulsive (n = 96); 17% of the entire sample scored in the problematic range for sexual compulsivity. Data analysis of the four groups indicated statistically significant differences on descriptive characteristics such as gender, sexual orientation, relationship status, and occupation. In addition, patterns of use differed across groups including the primary method of pursuing sexual materials, primary location of accessing sexual material, and the extent to which cybersex has interfered with a respondent's life. This study is one of the few quantitative examinations of the patterns of problematic and compulsive use of the Internet for sexual purposes. Implications and suggestions for research, public education, and professional trainings are presented.

INTRODUCTION

Given its burgeoning growth and wide accessibility, the Internet or World Wide Web (WWW) is altering patterns of social communication and interpersonal relationships. An estimated 9 to 15 million people access the Internet

Address correspondence to Al Cooper, Ph.D., San Jose Marital and Sexuality Centre, 100 N. Winchester Blvd., Suite 275, Santa Clara, CA 95050, USA. E-mail: AlCooper@stanford.edu each day at a rate which is growing by an estimated 25% every three months (Cooper, 1998a; Fernandez, 1997; Computerworld, 1998). Internet users spend an average of about 9.8 hours per week visiting the more than 200 million web sites now in existence (Computerworld, 1998). An estimated 94 million individuals will have access to the Internet in the year 2001.

Sexuality is one aspect of human social behavior that is being dramatically impacted by the Internet. In fact, sex is reported to be the most frequently searched topic on the Internet (Freeman-Longo & Blanchard, 1998), and the pursuit of sexual interests on the Internet, or "cybersex," is a remarkably common activity for users. In April 1998 approximately nine million users (15% of the online population) accessed one of the top five "adult" web sites (Cooper, Scherer, Boies, & Gordon, 1999). This does not include the numerous other adult web sites, nor other Internet modalities which can be used for sexual pursuits (e.g., e-mail, news groups, and chat rooms) and a different sampling of online users in August 1999 found that 31% of the total online population visited an adult web site (Leone & Beilsmith, 1999). Cooper (1998a) suggested that there are three primary factors which "turbocharge" online sexuality and make it such an attractive venue for sexual pursuits. He called these the "Triple-A Engine," and they include accessibility (i.e., millions of sites available 24 hours a day, 7 days a week), affordability (i.e., competition on the WWW keeps all prices low and there are a host of ways to get "free" sex), and anonymity (i.e., people perceive their communications to be anonymous).

Clearly the Internet can be used for healthy sexual expression. For example, the Internet offers the opportunity for the formation of online or virtual communities where isolated or disenfranchised individuals (e.g., gay males and lesbians) can communicate with each other around sexual topics of shared interest (Cooper, Boies, Maheu, & Greenfield, in press) . Newman (1997) noted the educational potential of the Internet, citing the greater availability of information about sexuality and the potential for more candid discussions of sexuality online. The Internet may also be used to find romantic partners. Cooper and Sportolari (1997), in a discussion of "computer mediated relating," pointed out how in e-mail relationships there is less emphasis on physical attractiveness relative to more traditional face-to-face relationships. In addition, the Internet may allow for sexual experimentation in a forum that seems "safer," possibly facilitating identity exploration and development (Leiblum, 1997).

At the same time, some researchers have suggested that the use of the Internet for sexual purposes may be counterproductive to normal, healthy sexual development in certain individuals. Van Gelder (1985) warned of the potential for the Internet to be used as a means of obtaining child pornography, for contacting children for sexual purposes, and for assuming false identities in sexually oriented communications. Durkin and Bryant (1995) studied criminal and deviant use of the Internet and posited that the instant gratification of online communication provided a reinforcement for the operationalization of sexual fantasies that would otherwise be extinguished. Others have noted the danger of individuals neglecting their real-world relationships by spending increasing amounts of time engaged in "pseudointimate" online relationships (Cooper et al., in press). Anonymity, accessibility, and affordability (Triple-A Engine) seem to increase the chances that the Internet will become problematic for those who either already have a problem with sexual compulsivity or those who have psychological vulnerabilities rendering them at risk for developing such compulsivity. Researchers investigating the addictive potential of the Internet—with regard to both sexual and non-sexual use—have noted correlations between time spent online and negative consequences reported by users (Bingham & Piotrowski, 1996; Cooper, Scherer, et al., 1999; Young, 1996; Young & Rogers, 1998).

Indeed, the Internet, like other technologies, has both costs and benefits. Some investigators have argued the importance of online sexual behavior as a continuum extending from adaptive to problematic (Cooper, Scherer et al., 1999; Leiblum, 1997). Cooper, Putnam, Planchon, and Boies (1999), in their recent survey of 9,177 Internet users, found that while 43% of the respondents spent less than one hour per week in online sexual pursuits, at the same time approximately 8% spent 11 hours or more per week engaged in such activity. These data suggested that the majority of users who pursued sexual interests on the Internet were capable of limiting the time spent in these activities to reasonable levels but that some were having clear problems. Cooper, Putnam et al. (1999) put forth a theoretical model based on this "continuum model" describing three categories of people who use the Internet for sexual pursuits. These include *recreational users* who access online sexual material more out of curiosity or for entertainment purposes and are not typically seen as having problems associated with their online sexual behavior. Next there are *sexual compulsive users* who, due to a propensity for pathological sexual expression, use the Internet as one forum for their sexual activities. And finally there are the *at-risk users* who, if it were not for the availability of the Internet, may never have developed a problem with online sexuality. For these people the power of anonymity, accessibility, and affordability (Triple-A Engine) interacts with certain underlying personality factors of at-risk users and leads to patterns and behaviors that, without intervention, may develop into online sexually compulsive behavior. Delmonico (1997) suggests that issues such as isolation and fantasy contribute to at-risk users becoming sexually compulsive.

As Internet usage continues to increase, more and more clinicians are encountering patients whose presenting problem either stems from or is manifestly online sexual compulsivity. As the public and professional awareness of cybersex usage is raised, it becomes increasingly important to understand, assess, and treat this phenomenon. Cooper, Boies et al. (1999) examined Internet sexual behavior through the use of an online survey which asked web site visitors about their online sexual behavior. One focus area was the amount of time individuals reported spending online. Approximately 8% of respondents (n = 9,177) reported engaging in online sexual activity 11 hours or more per week. This group reported higher levels of distress around their online pursuits than other respondents, and seemed representative of those individuals whose online sexual activity was problematic and potentially compulsive.

Because the amount of time spent online represents only one dimension upon which to identify individuals who may be sexually compulsive it was decided that it would be valuable to expand the criteria to include some of the others factors generally accepted as important dimensions on which to identify sexual compulsivity. These include increased appetite, desire, or tolerance (contributing to increased time engaged in the activity); harm to self or others; denial or minimization of negative consequences; repeated attempts to stop or limit sexual behavior; repetition of behavior despite negative consequences; behavior interfering with social, academic, occupational, or recreational activities; obsession with the activity; and compulsion or loss of freedom in choosing whether to engage in a behavior (Cooper, 1998b; Carnes, 1991; Goodman, 1999; Schneider, 1994).

The purpose of this study was to increase our understanding of online sexual compulsivity by doing a second series of analyses of the data from the Cooper, Scherer, et al. study (1999) and using refined criteria for sexual compulsivity to identify the cybersex compulsives in the sample. As was mentioned earlier the original study based group assignment on the number of reported hours spent online for sexual pursuits, while this study used scores from the Kalichman Sexual Compulsivity Scale (SCS) (Kalichman, Johnson, Adair, Rompa, Multhauf, & Kelly, 1994) combined with time online, in order to identify the group of users displaying cybersex compulsivity. The SCS takes into account many of the characteristics of sexual compulsivity mentioned above; SCS items are summarized in Figure 1. Combining the criteria of time spent online in sexual activities with scores on the SCS affords the purest sample yet of individuals whose use of the Internet is sexually compulsive.

METHODS

This study was a more in-depth analysis of survey data that had been previously collected by the lead author in a 1998 study. For a more complete description of the methodology of the original study, the reader is referred to the methods section of the earlier article (Cooper, Scherer et al., 1999).

The Survey

GENERAL INFORMATION. The following personal demographics were gathered: age, gender, occupational status, sexual orientation, relational status, and the total weekly amount of time individuals go online.

My sexual appetite has gotten in the way of my relationships.

My sexual thoughts and behaviors are causing problems in my life.

My desires to have sex have disrupted my daily life.

I sometimes fail to meet my commitments and responsibilities because of my sexual behaviors.

I sometimes get so horny I could lose control.

I find myself thinking about sex while at work.

I feel that my sexual thoughts and feelings are stronger than I am.

I have to struggle to control my sexual thoughts and behavior.

I think about sex more than I would like to.

It has been difficult for me to find sex partners who desire having sex as much as I want to.

FIGURE 1. Kalichman Sexual Compulsivity Scale questions.

ONLINE SEXUAL PURSUITS. A number of questions were designed to assess online sexual behavior. Individuals were asked to report the weekly number of hours they go online for sexual pursuits using a ratio scale. They were also asked to indicate where they go online (home, work, both, or other) and what medium they most use online (e.g., e-mail, chat room, news groups, or WWW). Using a Likert scale, respondents were asked to rate the frequency of specific sexual pursuits behaviors, their preoccupation with being online, some of the feelings they experience while online, and the degree to which they present themselves differently than the way they actually are. Three questions were designed to assess self-perception of deleterious effects on the respondents' lives: whether respondents keep the time spent online a secret, how it interferes with their lives, and what aspect of their lives are jeopardized, if any, by their behavior.

SEXUAL COMPULSIVITY SCALE. Included as part of the survey was this 10-item measure of sexual compulsivity developed by Kalichman et al. (1994). Their analyses found that the scale had an alpha coefficient of .89 and temporal stability (test-retest coefficient of .95).

SEXUAL SENSATION SEEKING SCALE (SSSS). Also included was this 10-item measure developed by Kalichman et al. (1994), assessing the propensity to engage in novel or risky sexual behaviors. It has been shown to be highly internally consistent (Cronbach's alpha = .75) and to have temporal stability (test-retest coefficient = .78). It was also correlated with self-reports of engaging in risky sexual behaviors by gay men (Kalichman et al., 1994) as well as inner city men and women (Kalichman & Rompa, 1995).

Nonsexual Sensation Seeking Scale (NSSS). This 10-item scale was developed to assess thrill and adventure seeking, experience seeking, disinhibition, and susceptibility to boredom. Kalichman et al. (1994) reconfirmed its reliability (Cronbach's alpha =.79) and temporal stability (test-retest coefficient = .78).

Data Collection

In the original study, a 59-item survey was made available via the MSNBC web site in March and April 1998 for a period of seven weeks. Informed consent was provided, as well as information about confidentiality and anonymity with regard to survey responses. In addition to the regular MSNBC audience, a variety of major television and radio networks and newspaper interviews helped promote wider participation in the study. All surveys were completed interactively via the web site and submitted electronically.

In order to help insure against multiple submissions of a completed survey by the same respondent, the MSNBC server assigned a globally unique identifier (GUID) to each subject. This GUID number helped prevent participants from submitting multiple surveys. Despite these precautions, it nonetheless remains possible that a determined respondent might have made multiple submissions from different computers; although it is highly unlikely that with the large numbers of total subjects these responses would have affected the overall results to any significant degree.

As a statistical check of external validity, comparisons were made to determine if the respondents were representative of other Internet users. The sample was compared to the 3.8 million visitors to the MSNBC web site in April 1998 (Goldberg, 1998). In addition, the sample was compared to the demographics of the 9.6 million visitors to the top five most frequently visited sexually oriented web sites. In both cases, it was concluded that demographics from the original sample were representative and comparable to both groups in a number of important, predictable ways.

For purposes of the present study, all of the original data that was collected was restored for a total working sample of 13,529. Subjects were eliminated if items were missing or inconsistent. If multiple submissions were detected, the first submission was retained and all other submissions were eliminated. This procedure diverged from the original data analysis and as a result, the final sample size is slightly different. Subjects were also eliminated if they were below the age of 18 years or above the age of 90 years. Based on these criteria, the data analyses were performed on the remaining sample of 9,265 respondents.

Reanalysis of the Data

The Kalichman SCS was used to divide the sample into four groups. The mean SCS score for the sample was 17.63 and standard deviation 6.15. The four groups were nonsexually compulsive (NC), moderate SCS score (MSCS), sexually compulsive (SC), and cybersexually compulsive (CC). Before describing the criteria of inclusion in one of these four groups, a comment on terminology is in order. There continues to be debate over the most appropriate terms to use in identifying those with compulsive sexual behaviors. Suggestions include nonparaphilia-related disorders (Kafka, 1993), sexual impulsivity (Barth & Kinder, 1987), sexual compulsion (Coleman, 1986), and sexual addiction (Carnes, 1983). There is still not a clearly agreed upon definition, classification, or label. However, the resolution of this controversy is beyond the scope of this article and for both consistency and simplicity we will utilize the term "sexual compulsivity."

Nonsexually compulsive (NC). Subjects in this group scored below 23.78 on the SCS, which represents one standard deviation above the mean. It was operationally defined that subjects scoring below this cutoff were not in the sexual compulsivity range. A total of 83.5% of the subjects fell into this category.

Moderate SCS score (MSCS). Subjects in this group scored between 23.78 and 29.93 on the SCS, which represented between one and two standard deviations above the mean. Though we operationally defined sexual compulsivity as having an SCS score higher than two standard deviations above the mean, the scores in this group are far enough above the mean score such that members of this group are likely to have some degree of difficulties with sexual behaviors (and may in fact be sexually compulsive). A total of 10.9% of the subjects fell into this category.

Sexually compulsive (SC). Subjects in this group scored above 29.93 on the SCS, which represented two standard deviations above the mean. It was defined operationally that subjects scoring at this level would best be described as sexually compulsive. A total of 4.6% of the subjects fell into this category.

Cybersex compulsive (CC). The final group was composed of those who met the criterion for both sexual compulsivity (scoring above 29.93) on the SCS *and* who reported spending more than 11 hours per week in online sexual pursuits. Although only 1% of the subjects fell into this group, it is this strictly defined category that offers insight into the purest sample yet of what we have called the cybersex compulsive. These are the individuals who are not only assessed as sexually compulsive (as measured by the SCS), but who seem to use the Internet as an important part of their sexual acting out, much like a drug addict who has a "drug of choice."

RESULTS

Descriptive statistics and frequency tables were generated for the entire sample and all four subgroups. These data provide descriptive and detailed informa-

TABLE 1. Demographic Characteristics by Group Assignment

Variable	Nonsexually Compulsive (n = 7,738)	Moderate SCS Score (n = 1,007)	Sexually Compulsive (n = 424)	Cybersex Compulsive (n = 96)
Age (mean)*	35.33	33.44	32.57	33.50
Gender (%)*				
Male	86	89	88	79
Female	14	11	12	21
Orientation (%)*				
Heterosexual	87	86	85	63
Gay/Lesbian	7	5	6	16
Bisexual	6	9	9	21
Relationship (%)*				
Married	47	49	49	38
Committed	17	15	16	15
Single/Dating	18	17	12	26
Single/Not Dating	18	19	23	21

*Statistical significance ($p \leq .01$)

tion about selected variables. Table 1 presents basic demographic data across all four groups.

Demographics

A one-way analysis of variance (ANOVA) was performed on the subject's age to determine if there were statistically significant mean differences between groups. If significance was found, a univariate Scheffe post hoc analysis was applied in order to determine which groups were significantly different from one another.

A chi-square statistic was conducted on all demographic variables since they were nominal-level data.

The chi-square for gender indicated statistical significance ($p \leq .001$; $df = 3$). Upon examination, the cybersex compulsive group appeared significantly different from the other three groups. A significant gender shift was noted in the cybersex compulsive group in that women were more likely to be included in this group.

The chi-square statistic found significant differences between the groups on the variable of sexual orientation ($p \leq .001$; $df = 6$). The calculated percentages suggest that heterosexuals are less likely to be in the cybersex compulsive group, whereas homosexuals and bisexuals are more highly represented in that group, relative to the other three groups.

The chi-square statistic was also significant for relationship status ($p \leq .01$; $df = 9$). Again, the percentage change appeared most significant in the cybersex compulsive group as compared to the other three groups, with married respondents less likely to be in the cybersex compulsive group and respondents who were both single and dating more likely to be in the cybersex compulsive group.

Time Spent Online

Chi-square statistics were also applied to other nominal-level variables which were not demographic in nature. The survey items regarding amount of time spent online overall and the amount of time spent in online sexual pursuits asked subjects to choose from a range of categories. There were a total of ten categories varying from less than one hour per week to 80 or more hours per week and the mean scores provide some estimate of how these groups differed with regard to the total amount of time spent online and the amount of time spent pursuing sexual material online. Keep in mind that these estimates are interpolated from categorical data and only offer approximate times. While there is a clear distinction between the cybersex compulsive and the other three groups, it is important to remember that group assignment for the cybersex compulsive individuals was based on the amount of time they spent pursuing online sexual material.

The nonsexually compulsive group, the moderate SCS score group, and sexually compulsive group all reported spending approximately 15 to 25 total hours per week online overall. The cybersex compulsives reported spending an estimated average of about 35 to 45 total hours per week online overall. Similarly, the amount of time spent pursuing sexual material online is estimated at about 1 to 10 hours per week for the nonsexually compulsive group, the moderate SCS score group, and the sexually compulsive group, while the cybersex compulsives reported spending an estimated average of about 15 to 25 hours per week pursuing online sexual material. Thus, the cybersex compulsive group was overall online more than the other groups. It is unclear whether this was a cause or effect (or both) of their online sexual behaviors. Figure 2 presents the time spent online in sexual pursuits for the cybersex compulsive group in more detail.

Occupation

The groups were also analyzed by occupation. Subjects were divided into one of five occupational categories: professional (combining the categories professional, management, educator, and health care provider on the survey), computer field, student, at-home (homemakers and the unemployed), and other. These data are presented in Table 2. A chi-square analysis of the cybersex compulsivity group by occupation was statistically significant ($p \leq$ .001). Students appear more likely to be members of the cybersex compulsive group, whereas professionals and those in the computer field appear less likely to be in the cybersex compulsive group.

Location

Subjects were asked to identify the location from which they access online sexual material most frequently. The choices were home, work, both, or other locations. While groups differed on their reported location, one find-

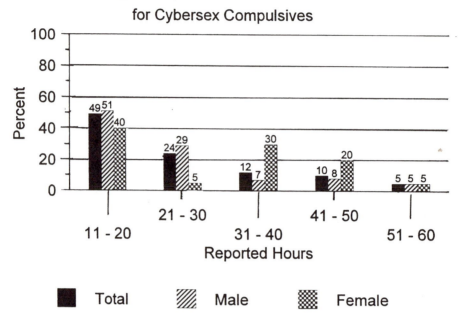

FIGURE 2. Sexual time spent online by cybersex compulsives.

ing of particular interest was that nearly 6% of the nonsexually compulsive subjects reported pursuing sexual material solely from work. These numbers increased across groups; 7% of the moderate SCS score group and 8% of the sexually compulsive subjects reported work being the only place they went online for sexual purposes. (The numbers of subjects using their work computers for some part of their cybersex activities are actually higher than these figures, in that these numbers do not include those who reported using both their work and home computers to access sexual materials.) This is as expected. Despite the small differences, there is a modest trend suggesting that as the severity of the problem increases, so does the person's need to have access to sexual stimuli, as well as their willingness to take risks with their jobs.

TABLE 2. Percent of Sample by Occupational Group

Occupation	Nonsexually Compulsive (n = 7,738)	Moderate SCS Score (n = 1,007)	Sexually Compulsive (n = 424)	Cybersex Addicts (n = 96)
Professional (%)	36	35	27	27
Computer Field (%)	24	24	21	19
At Home (%)	3	3	4	5
Student (%)	12	12	18	21
Other (%)	25	26	29	28

Statistically significant (p ≤ .001)

The data suggest that regardless of the degree of sexual compulsivity, 6% of employees use their work computer for sexual purposes about 1 to 10 hours per week.

Location of cybersex activities was further examined by gender, but gender did not appear to play a major role in determining use location. About 78% of males report using only their home computers for sexual pursuits and 6% reported using only their work computers. Similarly, 84% of females report using only their home computer, and 4% reported using only their work computer for sexual pursuits.

Online Behaviors

Cybersex activity includes a broad range of online behaviors. Delmonico (1997) suggested that there are three main categories of cybersex activity: pornography exchange, real-time discussions, and compact disk (CD-ROM) distribution. Subjects were asked which medium they used most to access online sexual material. Previous literature has suggested that there are significant gender differences associated with the online medium used (Cooper, Scherer et al., 1999). Table 3 examines the medium used, broken down by gender.

Here again we found that females tend to prefer chat rooms to other mediums and use the WWW as their second choice of online medium. Males prefer the WWW, with chat rooms as their second choice for the medium to engage in sexual pursuits. In looking at the cybersex compulsive group, the data generally supported the gender differences in online sexual pursuits with 70% of the female cybersex compulsives preferring chat rooms. Male

TABLE 3. Online Medium Used for Sexual Pursuits by Gender

Variable	Nonsexually Compulsive (*n* = 7,738)	Moderate SCS Score (*n* = 1,007)	Sexually Compulsive (*n* = 424)	Cybersex Addicts (*n* = 96)
Chat Rooms (%)				
Male	21.6	26.8	29.7	43.4
Female	48.1	53.3	46.0	70.0
E-mail (%)				
Male	7.6	9.0	8.3	9.2
Female	13.3	14.0	18.0	5.0
Newsgroups (%)				
Male	13.8	14.9	9.9	9.2
Female	3.1	1.9	0.0	0.0
World Wide Web				
Male	51.0	43.8	46.8	35.5
Female	22.9	21.5	20.0	10.0
Other (%)				
Male	6.0	5.6	5.1	2.6
Female	12.6	9.4	16.0	15.0

Statistically significant ($p \leq .001$)

cybersex compulsives tended to be more divided throughout the mediums; however, chat room and WWW usage continued to rank as their favored mediums. Females were significantly lower in their use of e-mail, which, as the most visible modality, may point up their desire to hide this type of behavior.

It is also interesting to note that no females in the sexually compulsive group or the cybersex compulsive group reported using newsgroups for sexual pursuits. Sexually related newsgroups are primarily for the exchange of erotic pictures and stories and are more comparable to e-mail than to chat rooms. This finding supported other literature that suggests women tend to desire cybersex in the context of a "relationship" rather than simply viewing erotic images or text (Cooper, Scherer et al., 1999; Carnes, 1991).

Gender Bending

A trend suggested by the media is the changing of demographic information while online for sexual pursuits. In fact, the practice is thought to be so widespread that the term "gender bending" has been used to describe individuals who switch gender while engaged in online sexual pursuits. Several questions on this survey asked subjects to identify if they changed certain characteristics when pursuing sexual material online. Despite popular beliefs, only 5% of the entire sample reported having ever changed their gender while online. However, the data suggested that it is common for people to misrepresent their age, with 48% of the subjects reporting they changed their age "occasionally" and 23% reporting they changed their age "often" or "too often." Surprisingly, 38% of the entire sample reported changing their race while online. Thus, we can say deceptive misrepresentation is, at least in this sample, a typical feature of online sexual pursuits.

The cybersex compulsive group does not differ markedly from the other three groups in terms of their propensity to misrepresent themselves online, although when examined across groups, there is more of a trend for changing one's age that appears to be associated with level of sexual compulsivity.

Secrecy

One aspect of sexually compulsive behaviors is the tendency to keep these activities secret. Subjects were asked whether they kept the amount of time they spent online for sexual pursuits a secret from others. The chi-square was significant ($p \leq .001$; $df = 3$) with the expected trend that nonsexually compulsive individuals were less likely to keep their cybersex activities a secret from others, as compared to the sexual compulsives and cybersex compulsives. Sixty-eight percent of the nonsexually compulsive group reported keeping their online sex time a secret from others and about 84% of the other groups reported the same. However, it is also apparent that, in general, keeping cybersex activities secret is important to subjects regardless of group assignment. This is not surprising as other sexual activities, whether or not compulsive, are also likely to be kept secret.

Interfering or Jeopardizing Aspects of Life

Two questions examined how pursuing online sexual materials may have interfered with or jeopardized certain aspects of respondents' lives. Overall, 32% of the entire sample identified at least one area of their life that has been negatively affected by their online sexual pursuits (e.g., personal, occupational, social, or recreational). When asked about jeopardizing a life area, 21% of all respondents reported that their online sexual pursuits had jeopardized an area of their life. In terms of ranking life areas, interference was reported most often in their personal life (12%) and relationships was the most common area jeopardized by online sexual pursuits (13%). Table 4 presents responses across all four groups for those who identified *all* areas of their lives affected or jeopardized, and those who identified *no* area of their life affected or jeopardized by use of online sexual material.

The general trend was that nonsexually compulsive individuals reported less interference and less jeopardizing of life areas than their moderate SCS score, sexually compulsive, and cybersex compulsive counterparts. Overall, these data corroborate earlier findings (Cooper, Scherer et al., 1999) that the majority of Internet users engage in sexual pursuits in ways that do not lead to difficulties in their lives, while a small but significant minority find that their activities create a great deal of problems.

Sensation Seeking

In addition to the Kalichman SCS, there were also scales which measured Sexual Sensation Seeking (SSS) and Nonsexual Sensation Seeking (NSS) behavior. On the SSS factor, all groups were significantly different from one another ($p \leq .001$), except that the sexually compulsive group was found not to be significantly different from the cybersex compulsive group. Both the sexually compulsive and the cybersex compulsive groups were significantly higher than the nonsexually compulsive and the moderate SCS score group.

TABLE 4. Percent of Sample Reporting Online Sex Interfering and Jeopardizing in Life Areas

Variable	Nonsexually Compulsive ($n = 7,738$)	Moderate SCS Score ($n = 1,007$)	Sexually Compulsive ($n = 424$)	Cybersex Addicts ($n = 96$)
All Areas (%)				
Interfere	1.4	6.2	14.9	24.0
Jeopardize	0.5	2.0	6.4	9.4
No Areas (%)				
Interfere	73.8	44.3	31.4	17.7
Jeopardize	83.0	64.8	46.7	28.1

Statistically significant ($p \leq .001$)

TABLE 5. Means Scores for Sexual Sensation Seeking (SSS) and Nonsexual Sensation Seeking (NSS) by Group

Variable	Nonsexually Compulsive (n = 7,738)	Moderate SCS Score (n = 1,007)	Sexually Compulsive (n = 424)	Cybersex Addicts (n = 96)
SSSS*	27.97	32.81	34.70	36.10
NSS*	23.51	26.63	28.74	28.17

*Statistically significant (p ≤ .001)

With respect to NSS scores, the nonsexually compulsive group was found to be significantly lower than all other groups, while the other three groups did not significantly differ from one another. Table 5 summarizes the mean scores for the SSS and NSS subscales.

Time Online for Sexual Pursuits (TOS)

In the original study, respondents to the survey were separated into 1 of 3 groups in the data analysis: low users, whose TOS was less than one hour per week; moderate users, whose TOS was 1 to 10 hours per week; and high users, with a TOS of 11 or more hours per week. In the present analysis, the cybersex compulsive group is comprised of those subjects both whose TOS was 11 or more hours per week *and* whose SCS scores were more than two standards above the mean. Of the 734 subjects with a TOS of 11 or more hours per week, only 96 were in the cybersex compulsive group.

We thought it was important to examine which groups the remaining 638 subjects fell into. There were none in the sexually compulsive group, since, operationally, any subject with an SCS score of more than two standard deviations above the mean and with a TOS of 11 or more hours per week was defined as being in the cybersex compulsive group. Four hundred ninety-four of the subjects with TOS of 11 or more hours per week were in the nonsexually compulsive group, and 144 were in the moderate SCS score group. These data are broken down by gender and presented in Table 6.

Though the 638 subjects in the high-user, noncybersex compulsive (HU/NC) category had low to moderate SCS scores, we wondered whether there was evidence that their being online 11 hours or more per week engaged in sexual pursuits either interfered with or jeopardized any aspects of their lives. In order to quantify this, we divided subjects into one of three categories: (a) subjects who reported no interference/jeopardy with any life area; (b) subjects who reported at least one life area affected/jeopardized; and (c) subjects who reported all five life areas listed in these two items on the survey as affected or jeopardized. When asked about interference with life areas, 54% of the HU/NC group reported experiencing no problems with life areas. However, 42% identified at least one life area affected, and 4% reported that all five life areas were affected by their online cybersex use. When asked about jeopardizing life areas, 72% of the HU/NC group re-

TABLE 6. Group Assignment of High Frequency Users (TOS ≥ 11 Hours per Week) by Gender

Variable	Nonsexually Compulsive (*n* = 494)	Moderate SCS Score (*n* = 144)	Cybersex Addicts (*n* = 96)
Total (%)	67.3	19.6	13.1
Male	67.4	20.4	12.2
Female	66.7	15.3	18.0

Statistically significant (p ≤ .001)

ported experiencing no jeopardizing of life areas. However, 27% identified at least one life area to have been jeopardized, and 1% reported that all five life areas had been jeopardized by their online activity.

DISCUSSION AND IMPLICATIONS

When considering our findings the reader is reminded that there are limitations of this study and that there are few other studies in this area to date. Thus, until a body of empirical research and replicated results are established all findings in this area need to be viewed with caution. Respondents to the survey were self-selected, and, as with any such survey, the possibility of a self-selection bias exists. Also, the cybersex compulsives in the group were identified on the basis of self-reported TOS and SCS scores. Since the SCS is a self-report measure, and denial of symptoms or concern can be a hallmark of sexual compulsivity, it is likely that there were cybersex compulsives in the sample that were not identified. At the same time, the large sample size and conservative statistical and methodological approach give us confidence that future research will corroborate many of our findings. Our study highlights the value of conducting online research in better understanding various facets of human sexuality. In addition, the dearth of almost any substantial research in the area of Internet sexuality make this study enormously important for those interested in an empirically based theoretical understanding, as well as clinical formulations, of online sexual compulsivity.

A Purer Sample of Cybersex Compulsives

Though the focus of this article is sexually compulsive behavior on the Internet, it bears reiterating that one of our major findings was that for the vast majority of respondents, surfing the Internet for sexual pursuits did not lead to significant difficulties in their lives. This was supported by findings that for most of the respondents their online sexual activity neither interfered (68%), nor jeopardized (79%), any aspect of their lives. At the same time, for approximately 1% of the sample (i.e., cybersex compulsives) online sexual activity is clearly problematic and seems to have major deleterious consequences in their lives. In this group 82% reported that their cybersex activities interfered with some aspect of their lives, and 72% said it actually jeopardized some facet of their lives. In addition, in terms of those respondents who were indicating some degree of sexual compulsivity, we found a full 17% of the sample were significantly above the mean by one standard deviation. Of that 17%, 6% were found to be at least two standard deviations above the mean.

Understanding the High TOS, NC Group

In the original study, 8.3% of the respondents reported their TOS as 11 or more hours per week, whereas in the present study, only about 1% of the subjects were in the cybersex compulsive group. Hence, we wondered how to explain and categorize the remaining 7+ percent of subjects with a TOS of 11+ hours/week. The sexually compulsive group had no one with a TOS of 11+ hours/week because of the way this group was defined. Four hundred ninety-four (67.3%) of these subjects were in the nonsexually compulsive group, while an additional 144 (19.6%) of these subjects were in the moderate SCS (MSCS) score group and thereby acknowledging a fair amount of concern about their sexuality. A less conservative definition might well categorize them as being cybersex compulsives. Similarly others in their lives might see their problems as more serious then they do.

The HU/NCs are even more interesting and likely to have varied reasons for falling into this group. For example, a significant portion (possibly between 27–42%) are likely to be in denial about the true severity of their issues. This type of denial is fairly typical in those with sexual acting out issues and is supported by our findings that despite scoring within normal limits on the SCS, 42% still identified interference in at least one life area (with 4% reporting all five life areas) and 27% identified at least one life area to have been jeopardized (with 1% reporting all five life areas).

Other portions of this group may be comprised of those in the early stages of developing a cybersex compulsion and thus not yet experiencing the levels of distress reported by those subjects more deeply entrenched in their compulsivity. And finally, it is likely that some percentage of this group is made up of those with a high TOS who truly do not have a problem with their online sexuality. Possibly, this latter group may have an unusually highly developed level of self-discipline and awareness of the potential dangers associated with the abuse of the Internet for sexual reasons. They may also have both personality and demographic variables that somehow help protect them (e.g., marital status, being a little older, working with computers).

Sexually Disenfranchised and At-Risk Groups

We compared the demographic characteristics of the cybersex compulsive group with the other groups of users in order to begin to develop some insight into the vulnerabilities that might put a user at risk for developing a cybersex compulsion. One noteworthy difference between the groups is seen when examining sexual orientation (chi-square $p < .001$, $df = 6$). Homosexual and bisexual respondents were clearly over represented in the CC (homosexual—16%; bisexual—21%) versus the NC (homosexual—7%, bisexual—6%) group. This is an intriguing finding but we must be cautious not to allow for simplistic explanations and instead realize this elevation is likely the result of a number of factors in combination. One being that bisexuals and homosexuals use the Internet more often than their heterosexual counterparts for experimentation and the expression of a variety of sexual behaviors. This is not surprising and indeed is even adaptive as anonymity, accessibility, and affordability (Triple-A Engine) provide a sense of safety and ready access to partners. In addition, different sexual norms and expectations, conflicted feelings about various aspects of homosexuality, as well as other cultural factors might lead to elevations on the SCS when in fact the respondent is not sexually compulsive (e.g., item 40: "My desires to have sex have disrupted my daily life," or item 46: "I think about sex more than I would like").

While the above cultural and contextual factors cannot be underestimated it should, at the same time, not be lost that gay and bisexual subjects in the cybersex compulsive group did in fact report highly elevated SCS scores, as well as significant distress relative to other respondents. Thus, it is possible to acknowledge discrimination, societal repression, and different cultural norms and still remain concerned that many of these people may not be in control of their sexual behaviors.

This again fits in to a theory that says that homosexuals and bisexuals (as well as other sexually disenfranchised groups) may be more at risk for online sexual compulsivity. The Internet has a number of potentially advantageous dimensions for these populations, in that it provides a venue for those who would otherwise be concerned about a host of negative repercussions to engage more freely in sexual pursuits. However, this freedom is a two-edged sword and can both enhance and damage the lives of those who avail themselves of it. Anonymity, accessibility, and affordability (Triple-A Engine) can pose a particular hazard for those users whose sexuality may have been suppressed and limited all their lives when they suddenly find an infinite supply of sexual opportunities.

This danger is dramatically illustrated by the recent report (Nieves, 1999) of an alarming number of syphilis cases over a two-month period in San Francisco. The investigation found that all cases originated in the same San Francisco gay male chat room on America Online. Combined, these seven men had 99 sexual contacts in the prior two months, and five of the seven were HIV-positive. Although we cannot say with total confidence that these men were truly sexually compulsive, it is hard to deny that they were engaging in risky behavior and that their Internet activity played a role in this.

We also found that women tend to have more difficulties with online sexual compulsion (chi-square, $p < .001$, $df = 6$, for gender distribution across the groups). While the ratio of men to women is 6.14, 8.09, and 7.33 in the nonsexually compulsive, moderate SCS, and sexually compulsive groups, respectively, it is 3.76 in the cybersex addict group. Clearly women are over-represented in this group, relative to the other groups. One explanation may be similar to that provided earlier if women are also thought of as a sexually disenfranchised population. Though the Internet offers women freedom from the constraints placed on their sexual expression by community standards and expectations regarding its "proper role" in their life, this freedom again cuts both ways, and carries with it increased risk for the development of problematic online sexual behaviors. Thus it would follow that as women more freely experiment and take sexual risks (Cooper, Scherer et al., 1999) in ever greater numbers it puts more of them at risk for developing a sexual compulsion.

Another explanation is that men are less likely to self-identify as having a problem (as manifested on the SCS scale) with online sexuality, while women are more willing to see these behaviors as problematic. This meshes with the fact that women are more likely to acknowledge a range of psycho-logical difficulties. In this situation, they may be even less prone to denial since it is harder for a female to "normalize" excessive time on the Internet (men are still more likely to use the Internet; in fact, 86% of our respondents were male), and/or because women are more likely (given prevailing social and gender-role expectations) to see using a computer for sexual pursuits as a problem.

Having such a large and diverse sample allowed us a window into small, often overlooked populations and how they interacted with online sexuality. One example is lesbians who were found to present an interesting contrast to some of the earlier findings and explanations. Despite lesbians being both female and homosexual (attributes which, when taken alone, were each overrepresented in the cybersex compulsive group) they were found to be underrepresented in the cybersex compulsive group. This result underscores the importance of considering lesbian sexuality as distinct from gay male sexuality in studies such as this, and raises the question as to what factors protect lesbians from developing cybersex compulsivity.

Another group less vulnerable to cybersex compulsion was those who were married. Reasons for this might be married people are either less likely to spend a great deal of time in cybersex pursuits, or perhaps simply less able to find the privacy to do so. Also plausible is that different dynamics lead a person to be either likely to get married or, alternatively, to develop an online sexual compulsion. Also of interest is that people who were both single and dating were more likely to be in the cybersex compulsive group. This makes intuitive sense when considering that people who are both single and dating are the subgroup most likely seeking sexual relationships, which might fuel a level of online sexual activity leading them to be more prone to problems with that behavior.

Workplace and Occupational Concerns

The findings concerning the location of cybersex activity and its prevalence at work were also striking. Although we did find that cybersex compulsives are more likely to use their work computers for cybersex activity (indicating a greater willingness to take risks), perhaps the most remarkable aspect of these findings was the extent to which subjects in all groups were apt to carry on cybersex activities at work. Even for the nonsexually compulsive group, 6 out of 100 employees reported their work computers to be the primary way they accessed sexual material. In addition, if we include respondents who reported using both work and home computers for sexual pursuits, then an amazing 20% of men and 12% of women are using their work computers for at least some portion of their online sexual activity. This corroborates data from other sources reporting that adult content sites are the fourth most visited category while at work (surpassed only by news/information/entertainment sites, search engines, and marketing and corporate information sites; Leone & Beilsmith, 1999), and that 70% of all adult content traffic occurs during the 9-to-5 workday (Branwyn, 1999). Once again anonymity, accessibility, and affordability (Triple-A Engine) provide vastly increased opportunities for people to engage in all types of sexual activities, and this is a frequent occurrence in the workplace. Ignoring the financial implications associated with these data for the moment, it is still somewhat striking to find a trend in which subjects across all groups report engaging in a behavior involving significant risk if discovered. This suggests that there may be a need for more workplace seminars on this subject in the same manner that business has educated employees about sexual harassment.

Additionally in terms of the impact on the workplace, the findings regarding the occupational status of respondents in the four groups were surprising. Approximately three fourths of respondents fell into one of four occupational groups: professionals, workers in the computer field, students, and an "at-home" category including both the unemployed and homemakers. Of these groups, only students were more likely to appear in the cybersex compulsive group, and thus they need to be considered another at-risk group. The combination of their increased access to computers, more private leisure time, and developmental stage often characterized by increased sexual awareness and experimentation are all reasons this group is more at risk for the development of cybersex compulsivity. In contrast, those in the computer field were at lower risk for cybersex compulsion for reasons that remain unclear at this point.

Additional Findings

Subjects in the nonsexually compulsive group, the moderate SCS score group, and the sexually compulsive group all tended to use the WWW and chat rooms most frequently, though women in these groups tended to favor chat rooms over the WWW and men tended to favor the WWW over chat rooms. However both male and female cybersex compulsives were more likely to use chat rooms; hence favoring an interactive modality in their sexual pursuits. It may be that the particularly engaging nature of chat rooms may be a "slippery slope" for certain at-risk individuals in the development of their cybersex compulsivity, or that certain individuals who habituate to less powerful forms of online sexual activities over time gravitate to chat rooms, or that chat rooms are a transitional step from online sexual interactions to meeting and finding face-to-face partners. In any case, the use of chat rooms for sexual pursuits should be a red flag and something to which clinicians should pay particular attention.

In addition, subjects in the cybersex compulsive group differed from the other three groups with regard to time spent online. Cybersex compulsives spent, on average, nearly twice the amount of time in general online activities as the other groups. They also spent twice as much time pursuing sexual material as the other groups, and about half of their online time solely in pursuit of sexual materials.

Examining the scores on the Kalichman scales was also informative. The cybersex compulsives and the sexually compulsive groups both scored significantly higher on the SSSS, and the nonsexual compulsives scored lower on the NSSS than the other three groups. This supports the notion that a propensity for sensation seeking—whether sexual or nonsexual—is an additional risk factor for cybersex compulsivity.

Summary and Implications

Our findings indicate that the majority of Internet users surveyed engage in cybersex activities for 10 hours or less per week (and roughly half of this group for less than one hour per week). In general, these pursuits do not interfere with the respondents' lives. Nonetheless, there is a small group of users (approximately 1%) for whom online sexual activity has clearly become a compulsive behavior, as well as a larger group (17%) who give some strong indication of problems with their sexual behavior.

Several demographic variables came to light as putting an individual at an increased risk for cybersex compulsivity. The reader is cautioned to keep in mind that this does not mean that these groups have any monopoly on being at risk, but only that they may be at increased risk. Both women and gay men were more highly represented in the cybersex compulsive group, and we believe that the sexual disenfranchisement of these two groups may play a role in their increased risk. Surprisingly those working in the computer field were not found more in the cybersex compulsive group, and of the various occupational groups examined, only students emerged as at greater risk. The propensity to take risks both in sexual and nonsexual behavioral domains, consistent with previous research on other forms of sexual compulsivity, is also more common in cybersex compulsives. In addition, the use of chat rooms as well as the greater number of overall time online for sexual pursuits were both more frequently found for cybersex compulsives.

The following recommendations are based on the core assumption that fully 20–30% of online users visit sites and engage in online sexual activities. Thus, increased attention needs to be paid to the issue of Internet sexuality. In addition, as 20 million (and growing) people visit sexual sites each month, it is comforting to say that the vast majority will not experience any major adverse reactions from their sexual surfing. On the other hand, even if we use our most conservative estimate that 1% of this population have a fully blown cybersex compulsion we are talking about a minimum of 200,000 people with a brand new disorder. Imagine the furor if a new drug (like MDMA) appeared on the streets and counted 200,000 people as dependent in just a few years. This is a hidden public health hazard exploding, in part because very few are recognizing it as such or taking it seriously. Recommendations for learning more about this behavior are described below.

RESEARCH

This study points to the need for increased research (as well as the funding and support to make it feasible) on the developmental pathways of cybersex compulsivity. Two starting questions include which users are likely to be at risk, and what makes cybersex activities so highly problematic for these people. Just as important is distilling what factors fortify certain populations and enable them to engage in certain types of cybersex activities without it negatively impacting their lives or progressing to a repetitive and problematic behavior. Research in this area also needs to be conducted which investigates the relationship of cybersex compulsion to more traditional varieties of sexual compulsion and/or addiction. Carnes (1999) reported that 71% of sexual addicts reported experiencing trouble with some type of sexual activity on the Internet. Has the Internet "created" a new category of sexual compulsives, or has it simply provided the already existing sexual compulsive an additional way to act out their behavior? Understanding this relationship between sexual compulsion and cybersex may be the first step in developing effective treatment models.

Finally, a critical question that needs to be addressed is whether, and to what extent, online sexual compulsivity translates into or facilitates potentially damaging behavior offline. For example, the question of whether individuals who engage in online pedophilic pursuits are more or less likely to ultimately engage in these behaviors offline.

PUBLIC EDUCATION

The data find a clear need for a dramatic increase in broad-based educational efforts on issues of cybersex, as well as sexually compulsive behaviors in general. These educational efforts should be aimed at raising public awareness to facilitate the development of other preventive measures. In addition to this primary avenue of prevention, secondary and tertiary prevention should also be addressed. These prevention strategies would include the development of interventions for users prone to develop cybersex compulsivity as well as for individuals who are attempting to gain control over what they acknowledge to be problematic behaviors. Since many individuals who struggle with one compulsive behavior often report other compulsive behaviors or addictions, these methods of education and prevention may be particularly important with the cybersex compulsives. One segment of this thrust would be to encourage seminars and focused discussions in schools, the workplace, and even in computer classes around both healthy and problematic uses of the Internet.

Enlisting the aid of the computer industry and Internet providers would provide the perfect time, place, and opportunity for those who profit from the public's interest in this technology to also take responsibility for warning users to the possible dangers. Clear warnings about the "potential hazards" of online sexuality could easily be delineated in their materials, analogous to that included with cigarettes, alcohol, firearms and other volitional activities that carry inherent risks (e.g., many gambling establishments participate in some level of public awareness of the difficulties that pathological gambling can pose to an individual and their family).

Similarly, in lieu of just outlawing adult-content web sites (and possibly driving them underground or offshore), an alternative would be to mandate their providing specific warnings, as well as links to other sites (e.g., the National Council of Sexual Addiction and Compulsivity) where users could get more information on warning signs, intervention strategies, and resources for treatment (when indicated).

Finally, the most effective medium by which to reach and influence the greatest numbers of people in our society is by getting the attention of the media. Their commitment to additional in-depth and empirically based explorations (as opposed to highlighting prurient and sensationalistic hype) of these issues would be an invaluable way for rapidly raising the public's awareness and providing them with an increased ability to determine whether a loved one, an employee, or they themselves have a problem with cybersex.

PROFESSIONAL TRAININGS

There is little doubt that there need to be many more opportunities for therapists to participate in comprehensive trainings in the assessment and treatment of patients presenting with problems related to online sexual behaviors and cybersex compulsion. Though more professionals are able to identify the manifestations of general sexual compulsivity, there remains a lack of awareness and information about sexual compulsivity on the Internet. As technology continues to advance, clinicians need to increase their skills in assessing for cybersex compulsion and the constantly evolving ways that clients engage in sexual behaviors while online. Ways to enhance these skills might include reading articles (such as those in this journal), attending specific trainings at conferences, and/or taking relevant online continuing education courses.

As our research indicates, clinicians need to rely on more than just self-report for their determination of whether the patient is a cybersex user, abuser, or compulsive, and what other collateral problems may exist for that client. Familiarity with literature from a variety of fields, including addictionology and sexology is essential in assisting therapists in learning how to better deal with issues ranging from spotting cyberinfidelity, identifying and treating cybersexual compulsion, and how best to intervene with the sexual curiosity of young people and their access to the Internet. Familiarity with current models of treatment for sexual addiction and compulsivity will play a significant role in successful treatment of cybersex compulsives. One option for intervention is the 12-Step recovery groups for sexual addiction and/or compulsivity. These groups often assist clients in modifying their compulsive sexual behaviors and interpersonal relationships. Clinicians should be familiar with the 12-Step groups that are available as an adjunct to individual and group therapies. Trainings will both need to help the therapists transfer extant knowledge and interventions from work with other sexual acting out problems to the online world, as well as identifying and developing methods specifically geared to cybersex issues.

For example, one issue that was presented and supported in this research is the concept of the "Triple-A Engine" (Anonymity, Accessibility, and Affordability) which fuels cybersex compulsion (Cooper, 1998a). Clinicians may want to focus interventions on these Triple-A events in order to reduce the power of these factors in maintaining the cybersex cycle. (For a detailed explanation of how this might be done see Cooper, Putnam et al., 1999.)

SUMMARY AND CONCLUSIONS

This article presents new data on cybersex users, abusers, and compulsives. These finding were presented to help clinicians and researchers better understand the individuals using the Internet for sexual purposes, who might be most at risk for developing problems associated with this behavior, and how to determine if intervention may be required. Suggestions were made for further research and ways to increase public and professional awareness of the complex behaviors that often accompany cybersex compulsion.

There is little doubt that use of the Internet will continue to explode. As people spend more time online and look to the Internet to fulfill an ever increasing amount of their sexual needs, the issues associated with online sexuality will become increasingly important and salient. We need to be involved in helping to educate the public, as well as other professionals, as to the ways that this new technology and venue can be used to enhance their lives and sexual relations, as well as to warn them as to the myriad ways that these modern day Sirens could, in fact, be luring them toward the rocks.

REFERENCES

Barth, R. J., & Kinder, B. N. (1987). The mislabeling of sexual impulsivity. *The Journal of Sex and Marital Therapy, 13*(1), 15–23.

Bingham, J. E., & Piotrowski, C. (1996). On-line sexual addiction: A contemporary enigma. *Psychological Reports, 79,* 257–258.

Branwyn, G. (1999, March 12). How the porn sites do it. *The Industry Standard.* [Online]. Available: http//www.thestandard.net

Carnes, P. (1983). *Out of the shadows: Understanding sexual addiction.* Minneapolis, MN: CompCare.

Carnes, P. J. (1991). *Don't call it love: Recovery from sexual addiction.* New York: Bantam Books.

Carnes, P. J. (1999). Editorial: Cybersex, sexual health, and the transformation of culture. *Sexual Addiction & Compulsivity, 6*(2), 77–78.

Coleman, E. (1986). Sexual compulsion vs. addiction: The debate continues. *SIECUS Report, 14*(6), 7–11.

Computerworld. (1998). *Commerce by numbers—Internet population* [Online]. Available: http://www.computerworld.com/home/Emmerce.nsf/All/pop

Cooper, A. (1998a). Sexuality and the Internet: Surfing into the new millennium. *CyberPsychology & Behavior, 1*(2), 181–187.

Cooper, A. (1998b). Sexually compulsive behavior. *Contemporary Sexuality, 32*(4), 1–3.

Cooper, A., Boies, S., Maheu, M., & Greenfield, D. (1999). Sexuality and the internet: The next sexual revolution. In F. Muscarella & L. Szuchman (Eds.), *The psychological science of sexuality: A research based approach* (pp. 519–545). New York: Wiley.

Cooper, A., Putnam, D. E., Planchon, L. A., & Boies, S. C. (1999). Online sexual compulsivity: Getting tangled in the net. *Sexual Addiction & Compulsivity, 6*(2), 79–104.

Cooper, A., Scherer, C., Boies, S. C., & Gordon, B. (1999). Sexuality on the internet: From sexual exploration to pathological expression. *Professional Psychology: Research and Practice, 30*(2), 154–164.

Cooper, A., & Sportolari, L. (1997). Romance in cyberspace: Understanding online attraction. *Journal of Sex Education and Therapy, 22*(1), 7–14.

Delmonico, D. L. (1997). Cybersex: High tech sex addiction. *Sexual Addiction & Compulsivity, 4*(2), 159–167.

Delmonico, D. L., & Griffin, E. (1997). Classifying problematic sexual behavior: A working model. *Sexual Addiction & Compulsivity, 4*(1), 91–104.

Durkin, K. F., & Bryant, C. D. (1995). "Log on to sex": Some notes on the carnal computer and erotic cyberspace as an emerging research frontier. *Deviant Behavior: An Interdisciplinary Journal, 16,* 179–200.

Fernandez, E. (1997, April 6). The new frontier: Net sex. *San Francisco Examiner,* p.14.

Freeman-Longo, R. E., & Blanchard, G. T. (1998). *Sexual abuse in America: Epidemic of the 21st century.* Brandon, VT: Safer Society Press.

Gaither, G. A., Franklin, M. D., Hegstad, H. U., & Plaud, J. J. (1997, August). *The sexual sensation seeking scale: Relationships to other sexuality measures.* Paper presented at the 105th annual conference of the American Psychological Association, Chicago, IL.

Goldberg, A. (1998). *Monthly Users Report on MSNBC for April 1998.* Washington DC: Relevant Knowledge.

Goodman, A. (1999). *Sexual addiction: An integrated approach.* Madison, WI: International Universities Press.

Kafka, M. P. (1993). Update on paraphilias and paraphilia-related disorders. *Currents in Affective Illness, 12*(6), 4–8.

Kalichman, S. C., Johnson, R. R., Adair, V., Rompa, D., Multhauf, K., & Kelly, J. A. (1994). Sexual sensation seeking: Scaled development and predicting AIDS-risk behavior among homosexually active men. *Journal of Personality Assessment, 62,* 385–397.

Kalichman, S. C., & Rompa, D. (1995). Sexual sensation seeking and sexual compulsivity scales: Reliability, validity, and predicting HIV risk behavior. *Journal of Personality Assessment, 65,* 586–601.

Leiblum, S.R. (1997). Sex and the net: Clinical implications. *Journal of Sex Education and Therapy, 22*(1), 21–28.

Lennon, B. (1994). An integrated treatment program for paraphiliacs, including a 12-step approach. *Sexual Addiction & Compulsivity, 1*(3), 227–241.

Leone, S., & Beilsmith, M. (1999, February). *Monthly Report on Internet Growth.* Washington, DC: Media Metrix.

Newman, B. (1997). The use of online services to encourage exploration of ego-dystonic sexual interests. *Journal of Sex Education and Therapy, 22*(1), 45–48.

Nieves, E. (1999, August 25). Privacy questions raised in cases of syphilis linked to chat room. *New York Times,* p. 1.

Schneider, J. P. (1994). Sex addiction: Controversy within mainstream addiction medicine, diagnosis based on the DSM-III-R and physician case histories. *Sexual Addiction & Compulsivity, 1*(1), 19–44.

Schwartz, M. F. (1994). The Masters and Johnson treatment program for sex offenders: Intimacy, empathy, and trauma resolution. *Sexual Addiction & Compulsivity, 1*(3), 261–277.

Swisher, S. (1995). Therapeutic interventions recommended for treatment of sexual addiction/compulsivity. *Sexual Addiction & Compulsivity, 2*(1), 31–39.

Van Gelder, L. (1985, October). The strange case of the electronic lover. *Ms.,* pp. 94, 99, 101–104, 117, 123–124.

Young, K. S. (1996). *Internet addiction: The emergence of a new clinical disorder.* Paper presented at the 104th Annual Convention of the American Psychological Association, Toronto, Canada.

Young, K. S., & Rogers, R. C. (1998). The relationship between depression and Internet addiction. *CyberPsychology & Behavior, 1*(1), 25–28.

Chapter 2

Effects of Cybersex Addiction on the Family: Results of a Survey

JENNIFER P. SCHNEIDER

Arizona Community Physicians, Tucson, Arizona, USA

A brief survey was completed by 91 women and 3 men, aged 24-57, who had experienced serious adverse consequences of their partner's cybersex involvement. In 60.6% of cases the sexual activities were limited to cybersex and did not include offline sex. Although not specifically asked about this, 31% of partners volunteered that the cybersex activities were a continuation of preexisting compulsive sexual behaviors. Open-ended questions yielded the following conclusions:

1. *In response to learning about their partner's online sexual activities, the survey respondents felt hurt, betrayal, rejection, abandonment, devastation, loneliness, shame, isolation, humiliation, jealousy, and anger, as well as loss of self-esteem. Being lied to repeatedly was a major cause of distress.*
2. *Cybersex addiction was a major contributing factor to separation and divorce of couples in this survey: 22.3% of the respondents were separated or divorced, and several others were seriously contemplating leaving.*
3. *Among 68% of the couples one or both had lost interest in relational sex: 52.1% of addicts had decreased interest in sex with their spouse, as did 34% of partners. Some couples had had no relational sex in months or years.*
4. *Partners compared themselves unfavorably with the online women (or men) and pictures, and felt hopeless about being able to compete with them.*

I would like to thank David Delmonico for doing the statistical analysis for this study. Also my gratitude to the following therapists who may have distributed the survey online and to appropriate clients, and apologies to those who did so but whom I neglected to thank: Judy Burch, Patrick Carnes, Deborah Corley, Joyce Dohanian, Patsy Fargason, Reid Finlayson, Linda Hudson, Sandra Kline, Mark Laaser, Rhonda Milrad, Sharon O'Hara, Carol Ross, Carol Thompson, Doug Weiss, Rob Weiss, and Julie Wells.

Address correspondence to Jennifer P. Schneider, M.D., Ph.D., 1500 N. Wilmot, B-250, Tucson, AZ 85712, USA. E-mail: jschndr@azstarnet.com

5. *Partners overwhelmingly felt that cyberaffairs were as emotionally painful to them as live or offline affairs, and many believed
   that virtual affairs were just as much adultery or "cheating" as
   live affairs.*

6. *Adverse effects on the children included (a) exposure to
   cyberporn and to objectification of women, (b) involvement in
   parental conflicts, (c) lack of attention because of one parent's
   involvement with the computer and the other parent's preoccupation with the cybersex addict, (d) breakup of the marriage.*

7. *In response to their spouses' cybersex addiction, partners went
   through a sequence of prerecovery phases which consisted of
   (a) ignorance/denial, (b) shock/discovery of cybersex activities,
   and (c) problem-solving attempts. When their attempts failed
   and they realized how unmanageable their lives had become,
   they entered the crisis stage and began their own recovery.*

INTRODUCTION

*It felt like there was another woman or a "something" there that was com-
peting for his attention. I felt like he was choosing between me and "it,"
and "it" usually won. I felt that I should have been first in his heart, but "it"
was. I guess that I was a coaddict, as I considered sex and love as the same,
and when he was choosing the computer, he was rejecting me. When I was
home nights, and he would finally come to bed, then say he was too tired,
I would try to interest him, and when I was unsuccessful, I would go into
the living room and cry for hours.*

*He said that the computer was only a small part of the sex addiction,
that pornography and meeting other people was a greater part, but the
computer was an object that I could see, and, I guess, hate. When he was
away from home, he could make up excuses for what he was doing, but
when he was sitting in front of the computer and conversing for hours,
there was no doubt what he was doing.*

*The kids knew what was going on, to an extent. My son says there is no
way that he can trust his dad, but my son also has been visiting porn sites,
until we found out and talked to him about it.*

*I resented the computer for years, until I finally accepted the fact that
it was the user, not the machine that was causing the problem.*

—41-year-old woman, married 23 years

*I knew my husband was masturbating all the time, but I thought it was my
fault. When I found the computer disk going back five years, everything
made sense. I had been in denial about how much I knew, and how much
my life was out of control. I feel very used and violated because of this
behavior, and I have lost my trust.*

My husband would blame me when I would catch him masturbating at the computer. He would not do any chores when I was out; when I returned, he would throw the blinds and turn off the light really fast. He would keep looking at his pants to see if I could tell he had an erection. He would run out of the bedroom like he was just changing. He would call me and say he was coming right home at 4:00, and not show up until 7:00. He would say he was working really hard and not to give him a hard time.

I knew he would be masturbating if I left the house. I never said no to sex unless he was wasted drunk, I was not feeling well, or I was working. I believed that if I had sex more often, or if I were better at sex, he would not masturbate as much. I surveyed my friends to see if they'd caught their husbands masturbating, to see how often they thought it was normal to masturbate, to see what kind of sex they had with their husbands and how often.

I thought I was not good enough because I did not look like the girls in the pictures. I thought that if I dressed and looked good it would keep him interested. I would give up competing with his masturbating and not want to have sex with him. I would not walk into the room at night because I did not want to walk in on him.

If the kids and I were coming home from somewhere and his car was there, I would run into the house first and be loud so the kids would not walk in on him. I found semen on my office chair and pubic hair on my mouse. I would get dressed fast so I would not have to have sex with him. I stopped making dinner because I would not know when he would be coming home. I would have to mentally prepare myself for sex. I tried to talk with him about masturbation and how often he wanted to have sex. I was in denial about how unhappy I was.

My husband does not believe he has an addiction. He doesn't think it's a big deal because he says he was never with anyone else. He thinks all he needs is a more loving wife.

–38-year-old woman, married 15 years, divorcing

When I know that my husband has masturbated to cyberporn, I don't want him to touch me. I feel like I am leftovers, not first-run as I should be. My self-esteem is damaged beyond belief. To be honest, our sex life is pretty incredible—we are not prudes by any means. I just don't understand. How can it be soooo good for both of us but still not enough for him?

–31-year-old woman, married one year

The growth of the Internet in the past seven years has been phenomenal. Before 1993 the Internet was used by only a few persons in laboratories and universities. In 2001 there will be over 94 million users (Computerworld, 1998). Also increasing is the number of people who are drawn into using Internet access to obtain sexual satisfaction. Most of these people are "recreational users," analogous to recreational drinkers or gamblers, but a significant proportion have preexisting sexual compulsions and addictions that are now finding a new outlet. For others, with no such history, cybersex is the first expression of an addictive sexual disorder, one that lends itself to rapid progression, similar to the effect of crack cocaine on the previously occasional cocaine user.

In contrast to pornographic bookstores and theaters, involvement with prostitutes, exhibitionism and voyeurism on the street, purchase of pornographic magazines, and anonymous sex in hotels and parks, the Internet has several characteristics which make it the ideal medium for sexual involvement (Cooper, Putnam, Planchon, & Boies, 1999). It is widely accessible, inexpensive, legal, available in the privacy of one's own home, anonymous, and does not put the user at direct risk of contracting a sexually transmitted disease. It is also ideal for hiding the activities from the spouse or significant other (SO), because it does not leave obvious evidence of the sexual encounter. It takes some computer savvy on the part of the spouse to retrace the user's online adventures.

Other articles in this issue address the problem of compulsive cybersex involvement. The goal of this article is to describe how such behavior affects the SO and the children.

METHODS

To learn more about the effects of cybersex on the SO and family of the user, I employed the same qualitative research method used in previous studies of the effect of sex addiction on couples (Schneider, Corley, & Irons, 1998; Schneider & Schneider, 1990). The only difference was that the research was done entirely via e-mail, as I assumed that the target population would have access to a computer. A cover letter was sent to approximately 20 therapists who treat sex addicts, and they were asked to forward the letter to any persons they knew who were dealing with cybersex involvement in the family. The letter explained the nature of the research and invited the client to e-mail me to obtain a brief survey. The survey questions are listed in Table 1.

Because e-mail does not generally allow for anonymity, as a return address is automatically attached, I gave respondents the option of returning the survey to me via regular mail after cutting out any identifying information. Only 3 out of 94 respondents chose to respond via regular mail.

The survey asked questions both about the adverse effects of cybersex use on the partners and about their efforts at resolution of the problems, either individually or as a couple. This article addresses only the first part. When reading the overwhelmingly pained, discouraged, and negative comments of the SOs, it is helpful to know that many of the same writers later describe recovery from their codependency and their pain, whether or not they are still in the relationship. In a number of cases, the cybersex user is taking major positive steps toward recovery from the addiction, and the couple relationship has changed significantly for the better.

TABLE 1. Cybersex Survey for Partners

A. Demographics:
1. Your age?
2. Sex?
3. How long were/are you in the relationship with/married to the sex addict?
4. Are you still in the relationship?
5. How long (years, months, etc.) were/are online sexual activities by the addict a problem for you?
6. As far as you know, what activities did your partner's online sex addiction consist of?
7. To your knowledge, has your partner's online sex addiction led to actual sexual encounters with other people?

B. Effects on you:
1. How did your partner's Internet sexual behaviors affect you (emotions, relationship, money, sex, family, codependent behaviors, etc.)?
2. Specifically, how have your partner's Internet sexual activities affected your sexual relationship with your partner?
3. Some sex addicts' online sex addiction leads to actual sexual encounters with other people. Other Internet sex addicts never have physical contact with other people in connection with the online sexual activities. If your partner is in the latter category, how would you respond to people who say, "What's the big deal about cybersex? After all, you're not risking catching any diseases from your partner, and your partner isn't actually cheating on you! What's the fuss?"
4. If you have children, how have they been affected by the cybersex addiction?

C. Efforts to deal with the situation
1. What have you done to try to cope with the effects of your partner's online sex addiction on you and your relationship? What are you doing now to cope?
2. If you're still in the relationship, what are you and your partner doing together to resolve any problems with your "sexual" relationship?

D. Please add any other comments which you think might be helpful to us in understanding how cybersex addiction affects the couple and the family.

NOTE ON TERMINOLOGY

This survey of partners of cybersex users did not attempt to formally diagnose sex addiction in the (mostly) men described by the respondents, and by its nature represents only the perspective of the respondents. Any addictive disorder comprises loss of control (i.e., compulsive behavior), continuation despite adverse consequences, and obsession or preoccupation with the activity. It is likely that the vast majority of the cybersex users fulfill these criteria and indeed have an addictive sexual disorder. However, this study was not designed to ascertain this. Therefore, use of the term "cybersex addict" in this article is informal and should not be construed as a definitive medical diagnosis.

RESULTS

Demographics

Responses were obtained from 94 persons whose spouse or partner was heavily involved in cybersex activities. All responses were obtained within a 2-month period, in July and August 1999.

The 94 SOs comprised 91 women and 3 men. One woman and 2 men reported being in a homosexual relationship. The 94 cybersex addicts were 92 men and 2 women. The mean age of the 94 respondents was 38.0 +/– 7.9 years, with a range of 24–57. They had been in the relationship for a mean of 12.6 +/– 9.2 years and a range of 0.5–39 years. In response to the question, "Are you still in the relationship?" 74 (78.7%) replied yes, 9 (9.6%) no, and 11 (11.7%) were separated. That is, 21.5% were living apart. Several partners who were still living with the spouse stated that the marriage was essentially over and that they were planning to divorce.

The cybersex involvement had been a problem for the partners for a mean of 2.4 +/– 2.0 years and a range of 1 month to 8.5 years. Several, however, commented that although they had learned about the behavior very recently, they now recognized that it had been going on for a long time and was probably responsible for problems in the relationship whose nature they had not understood before.

What Partners Told About the Cybersex Addicts

SEXUAL ACTIVITIES

When asked about the addict's sexual activities, all responses included viewing and/or downloading pornography along with masturbation. Other behaviors were reading and writing sexually explicit letters and stories, e-mailing to set up personal meetings with someone, placing ads to meet sexual partners, visiting sexually oriented chat rooms, and engaging in interactive online affairs with same- or opposite-sex people, which included real-time viewing of each other's bodies using electronic cameras connected to the computer. Related activities included phone sex with people met online, and online affairs that progressed to real affairs. Several SOs knew that the addict was participating in unacceptable or illegal online activities such as sado-masochism and domination/bondage (5 reports), bestiality (2), viewing child pornography (1) and pornographic pictures of teenagers (6), and having sex with underage persons (1). One man reportedly signed on as a teenage girl and solicited lesbian sex, and another man posed as a teenage boy in teen chat rooms. Because the partners reported only those activities of which they were aware, it is reasonable to assume that the actual prevalence was higher.

LIVE OR OFFLINE SEXUAL ACTIVITIES

One might hypothesize that offline or live sexual encounters would be more problematic for a relationship than virtual encounters. Table 2 summarizes the responses to the question, "To your knowledge, has your partner's online sex addiction led to actual sexual encounters with other people?"

Compared with the 57 people who had reportedly not had offline affairs, the 28 who did have live affairs were on the average older (41.1 +/– 8.3

TABLE 2. Cyberaddicts' Live Sexual Encounters? (*N* = 94)

No	57	(60.6%)
Yes	28	(29.8%)
Unsure	9	(9.6%)

vs. 36.5 +/– 7.3 years) and had been in the relationship longer (15.2 +/– 10.0 vs. 10 +/– 8.8 years). Table 3 analyzes the relationship between marital status and offline involvement with other people. The percentages were calculated separately for each marital status group.

Because of the small numbers in the separated and divorced group, the differences are not statistically significant using the chi-square test, but the data do suggest that the likelihood of divorce is increased by this behavior. To the extent that the decision to divorce was related to the compulsive sexual behaviors, the data also show that cybersex even when others are not involved can have a significant negative impact on the viability of the marriage.

ONLINE SEX IS A CONTINUATION OF A PREEXISTING ADDICTIVE SEXUAL DISORDER

In 29 reports (30.9%) the cybersex activities were said to be a continuation of other compulsive sexual behaviors. Because some SOs may not have known about other behaviors, or may not have thought to mention them, this figure is likely to be an underestimate. Behaviors included phone sex, voyeurism, seeing prostitutes, and going to massage parlors. Most common was heavy involvement with pornography (magazines, videos, movies, etc.), often since the teen years.

PROGRESSION, INCLUDING LIVE SEX WITH OTHERS

A well-known characteristic of addictions is tolerance, which is the need to do more and more to get the same results. This may involve an increase in the quantity of the drug or behavior, or an escalation in the type of activity. For sex addicts, this may mean more hours on the Internet, a larger number of partners, or more bizarre or riskier activities, or going from vitual to actual sexual encounters.

TABLE 3. Effect of Having Live Sexual Encounters with Others on Current Marital Status (*N* = 94)

Marital status	Live sexual encounters with other people			
	Yes	Unsure	No	Total
Married	22 (29.7%)	7 (9.4%)	45 (60.9%)	74 (100%)
Separated	4 (36.4%)	1 (9.1%)	6 (54.5%)	11 (100%)
Divorced	4 (44.4%)	1 (11.1%)	4 (44.4%)	9 (100%)

Cybersex really accelerated the addiction on his part. It went from just magazines and movies (after his credit card was maxed out with phone charges) to spending hours on end on the computer looking at images, to hours on end chatting with anyone who would "talk." It took only 3 months to go from simple e-mail to all this, and he said it would have only been a matter of time before he did start to meet women in person had I not found the disk. [30-year-old woman who found a porn disk in the drive]

Sixteen respondents (17.6%) reported that their partner's cybersex activities had indeed progressed to live encounters with other people. In some cases these were people they met online in chat rooms, via e-mail, etc. In other cases, the computer sexual activity triggered other addictive behaviors which involved other people. For example, a gay man wrote that his partner's bathhouse activities with other people had increased. Women wrote that their husbands had begun new activities such as a sexual massage parlor, visits with prostitutes, the first real affair, or an additional affair.

Denial, minimization, and blame

Some SOs wrote that their spouses were now attending 12-step meetings for sex addicts and/or going to counseling. Many others, however, explained that their spouses did not believe they had a problem or, even if they did recognize this, were not motivated to do anything about it. Several SOs had separated, divorced, or were planning to leave because of their spouse's refusal to recognize the problem, go to counseling, or seek other help.

Effect of Addict's Cybersex Involvement on Partners

On the partner's emotions

Most SOs described some combination of devastation, hurt, betrayal, loss of self-esteem, mistrust, suspicion, fear, and a lack of intimacy in their relationship. Other responses were extreme anger or rage (two became physically abusive to their husbands), feeling sexually inadequate or feeling unattractive and even ugly, doubt one's judgment and even sanity, severe depression, and, in two cases, hospitalization for suicidality.

He put the porn and masturbation as a priority to sexual relations with me. I felt totally degraded, not much of a woman, not "good enough" for him. I felt betrayed, that he conned me into marrying him. He knew his actions were destroying our marriage, yet he lied to me continually. After I moved out, he swore to me that he would never "do porn again," only to continue it within a week of my returning. Without a doubt, the lies have been the worst. The second worst was seeing it happen. [41-year-old woman, still married]

This behavior has left me feeling alone, isolated, rejected, and "less than." Masturbation hangs a sign on the door that says "You are not needed, I can take care of myself, thank you very much." I have threatened, manipulated, tried to control, cried, gave him the cold shoulder, yelled, tried to be understanding, and even tried to ignore it. Denial and codependence are my character defects. [55-year-old woman, married 36 years]

Trust was a major casualty of the secrecy of cybersex addiction. Many SOs felt that this was at least as harmful to the relationship as the sexual activities themselves. Partners reported losing all trust in their mate and in anything he/she told them. Many reported that despite the addict's promises, "behavior has continued, but he has learned to be much more secretive about it." With each discovery, trust is further eroded. "Every time I walk into our 'office' area, I am fearful of what might appear on the screen." A common theme was, "The lies he told me concerning his whereabouts, while he looked me straight in the eye, have hurt worse than his having sex with them."

Three women reported having engaged in extramarital affairs or encounters, either to shore up their own self-esteem or else to get revenge on their spouses.

EFFECT ON THE SEXUAL RELATIONSHIP

A 34-year-old woman who had learned of her husband's cybersex involvement only weeks earlier, described the effects on the couple's sexual relationship:

I realize now that many of the things he most liked and requested when we made love were recreations of downloaded images. He is unable to be intimate, he objectifies me, he objectifies women and girls on the streets, he fantasizes when we're together. I feel humiliated, used, and betrayed, as well as lied to and misled. It's almost impossible for me to let him touch me without feeling really yucky and/or crying. I tried to continue being sexual with him initially (and in fact, being "more" sexual, trying to fix it by being sexier, better than the porn girls), and I couldn't do it. We have now been consensually abstinent for 3 weeks.

This description contains various themes that were brought up recurrently by survey respondents: a feeling of being objectified, comparing herself with the cybersex women, initial attempt to increase the quantity and/or variety of sexual activities, and a decreased desire to have sexual relations with the addict. This woman did not experience the most common complaint: Loss of interest by the addict in having sex with the partner.

Two thirds of respondents (68.1%) described sexual problems in the couple relationship that were generally related to the cybersex addict's sexual activities. In some cases these problems had resulted in decreased interest by the cybersex user in relational sex. In others it was the SO who had lost interest, and in some cases both partners had a decreased interest. As shown in Table 4, in only 30 (31.9%) coupleships were both partners still interested in sex with each other.

TABLE 4. Loss of Interest in Relational Sex (*N* = 94)

Cybersex user's relational sexual interest	Partner's relational sexual interest		
	Decreased	Not decreased	Total
Decreased	17 (18.1%)	32 (34.0%)	49 (52.1%)
Not decreased	15 (16.0%)	30 (31.9%)	
Total	32 (34.0%)		

When asked about the effect of cybersex on their sexual relationship, fully half of the 94 respondents (49, or 52.1%) said that their husbands were not interested, or hardly interested, in sex with them. Note that 32 of the 49 partners (65.3%) of those who had decreased sexual interest (34.0% of the entire group of 94 SOs) stated that they now have less sex than they want. The remaining 17 partners (18.1% of the entire group) reported that they too had shut down sexually, so that the lack of sexual activity at the time of reporting was mutual in 17 couples.

Additionally, 15 of the 94 partners (16%) reported that they were no longer interested in sex, although the cybersex addict was. In this group, it was the cybersex user who was still interested in relational sex, and was experiencing less sex with partner than the user wanted. In summary, 34% of the SOs complained that they were feeling deprived of relational sex, and another 16% of SOs reported that it was only the cybersex user who was unhappy with the lack of relational sex. In other words, according to the respondents, twice as many SOs as cybersex users wanted more sex with their relational partner than they were getting.

The SOs who were not interested in sex with the cybersex addict attributed their loss of interest primarily to their negative reaction to the Internet user's sexual activities with cybersex, phone sex, live encounters, etc. In total, half of the cybersex addicts and one third of the partners were no longer interested in marital sexual relations. This was reportedly not a problem for the addicts, who had substituted cybersex for sex with SO, but was definitely a problem for the partners, who felt angry, hurt, rejected, and often sexually unfulfilled.

Respondents who reported that the cybersex addict had been sexually compulsive (paper pornography, phone sex, etc.) even before the Internet came on the scene often stated that the couple's sexual relationship had been infrequent in those days as well. Some added that the problems in the sexual relationship had intensified since the cybersex activities began. Below are some examples of the reported problems.

CYBERSEX ADDICT ALONE HAS LOST INTEREST IN COUPLE SEX

Thirty-two respondents (34%) reported that although they still wanted a sexual relationship, the cybersex addict had withdrawn his sexual (and general) attention from the partner and family and devoted his (or her) time and energy instead to computer sex. Recurrent themes here follow:

- The partner felt hurt, angry, sexually rejected, inadequate, and unable to compete with cyberimages and sexy online women (or men) who were willing to do anything.
- The addict made excuses to avoid sex with the partner (not in the mood, too tired, working too hard, has already climaxed and doesn't want sex, the children might hear, his back hurts too much).
- During relational sex, the addict appeared distant, emotionally detached, and interested only in his/her own pleasure
- The partner ended up doing most or all of the initiating, either to get her/his own needs met, or else in an attempt to get the addict to decrease the online activities.
- The addict blamed the partner for their sexual problems.
- The addict wanted the partner to participate in sexual activities which she/he found objectionable.

> *Currently we have sex once every three months, usually only after I blow my stack and I suppose he feels obligated. Although I know that I am bright and attractive, emotionally I feel ugly, worthless, and unwanted by him or anybody else. For me the issue has not been the difference between him having e-mail sex or actual physical contact, it is that someone else is receiving his attention and I am not. I do many mental gymnastics in order to cope with this. In order to prevent becoming irritated with my partner because he rejects my sexual advances, I masturbate daily with the hope that it will prevent me from becoming "horny." Sometimes it works. I would not care at all if he masturbated online with a host of others, as long as I was an active part of his sex life.* [33-year-old gay male]

> *Since my husband was living in a fantasy world of Internet porn, I was the only one who initiated sex. I thought if I didn't we would never have sex and this would cause him to go elsewhere. He would respond but always seemed to be in another world during sex. When confronted with why he was not interested in sex, he said that "it was not as important to him as it is to other men."* [28-year-old woman, married 8 years]

> *He's not interested in sex with me and blames me. He told me it's his way or no way. He wanted me to participate with him on the net. He is up all night on the net and then is tired and unavailable. I feel like I'm making love to a corpse—he doesn't really participate.* [34-year-old woman, married 10 years]

PARTNER ALONE HAS LOST INTEREST IN COUPLE SEX

In 15 cases, the cybersex addict maintained his/her desire for sex with the SO, but the partner was less interested. In some cases the partner refused to have sex; in others, the partner didn't want to but continued out of fear of driving the addict further into online activities. Major themes reported follow.

- The partner's initial response in some cases was to increase the sexual activities in order to "win back" the addict. This early response was only temporary.
- The partner felt repelled and disgusted by the addict's online or real sexual activities and no longer wanted to have relationship sex.
- The partner could no longer tolerate the addict's detachment and lack of emotional connection during sex.
- The partner's anger over the addict's denial of the problem interfered with her/his sexual interest.
- In reply to pressure or requests by the addict to dress in certain ways or perform new sexual acts, the partner felt angry, repelled, used, objectified, or like a prostitute.
- Partner fears sex with the addict because the partner fears catching a disease from the addict, or has already caught one.

> *At first we had sex more than ever as I desperately tried to prove myself, then sex with her made me sick. I get strong pictures of what she did and lusted after, and I get repelled and feel bad. I used to see sex as a very intimate loving thing. We always had a lot of sex and I thought we were intimate. Now that I found out my wife was not on the same page, I can't be intimate or vulnerable—sex is now more recreational or just out of need.* [44-year-old man, married 26 years]

> *I was afraid of losing him. I began to try to compete with the images, being a sex toy. Then after a while, I began to feel like I didn't want to have sex anymore. I felt like I had to, but didn't want to.* [27-year-old woman, married 3 years]

> *I have felt for some time that I am not a part of his sexual activity, even while I am having sex with him. I feel cheap and used. I have no emotional connection with him except for the feelings of resentment, anger, and hopelessness.* [40-year-old woman, thinking of leaving the marriage after 20 years]

BOTH PARTNERS HAVE LOST INTEREST IN COUPLE SEX.

In 17 cases (18.1% of the 94 respondents), loss of interest by both partners put a virtual end to sexual relations between them. Typical dynamics were a man who was more interested in sex with the computer than with the wife, and a woman who felt rejected, angry, and unable to compete—i.e., a combination of the individual themes described earlier:

> *There was a time where we went four years with no physical contact, and right now it has been almost six months. The part of me that still feels a*

desire for him has a hard time overcoming the fact that he has to have these disgusting images in his head. I feel used and dirty, while at the same time I feel guilty because I know he is going through the motions because he does love me and he is trying to make me happy even though he'd rather not have sex with me.

COMPARISON WITH ONLINE SEXUAL PARTNERS

The knowledge that the addict's head is full of cybersex images inevitably produces in the SO a comparison between the spouse and the fantasy woman in terms of appearance, desirability, and repertory of sexual behaviors. Both addicts and partners were reported to make such comparisons. The SO feels she/he is competing with the computer images and people. ("If only I were perfect like his porn, then he would want the real thing and love me.") The result is often confusion—on the one hand, desire to emulate and better the cyberwoman (or man), on the other revulsion at the lack of intimacy and mechanical nature of the sex. Survey respondents reported vacillating between these two polarities.

His cybersex activities made me angry. They made me want to be more sexy and desirable, then at other times made me not want to have anything to do with him. It made me feel that when we were having sex and he closed his eyes, he was viewing some other person's body and therefore was not really "with" me. [48-year-old woman, married 4 years]

He's never been physically unfaithful, but he has had experiences with others. I feel cheated. I never know who or what he is thinking of when we are intimate. How can I compete with hundreds of anonymous others who are now in our bed, in his head? By chatting sex, he and others made up fantasies and pretended. How can reality ever satisfy him how? When he says something sexual to me in bed, I wonder if he has said it to others, or if it is even his original thought. Now our bed is crowded with countless faceless strangers, where once we were intimate. With all this deception, how do I know he has quit, or isn't moving into other behaviors? [34-year-old woman, married 14 years to a minister]

PARTNER INCREASES SEXUAL ACTIVITIES TO COMBAT THE PROBLEM

Some partners attempted a sexual solution to the cybersex addiction problem, typically either increasing the frequency of sexual activities with the addict, or else joining with the addict in his preferred activities:

I tried to initiate a variety of things I have seen in Penthouse. I feel ashamed of the things I've suggested, which I thought would change his behavior. I have to remind myself every day that that wasn't my normal behavior, and am trying to forgive myself. It's extremely difficult. [39-year-old woman, married 8 years, now divorced]

> *My husband is a minister who was stationed overseas for a year. We chatted daily, but never sexually. Then I learned about his cybersex activities, and felt cheated. Why wouldn't he ask me to have cybersex? I wasn't comfortable with this, but I thought I could "rescue" him. So we began a cybersex relationship. But much to my horror, he never quit with all the anonymous partners. So he lumped me together with all the online whores. When he returned, he continued his cybersex even though we were reunited.* [34-year-old woman, still in a long-term marriage]

WHAT'S THE BIG DEAL ABOUT ONLINE SEX?

This is the most common question that is asked by persons who focus on the absence of skin-to-skin contact during cybersex activities, and cannot understand why marriages actually break up over this issue. This question (see Table 1 for its language) elicited the most emotional and eloquent responses of the survey. Several themes were evident in the replies.

CONCERN ABOUT ESCALATION. Tolerance—the need to do more to get the same results—is a common feature of addictive disorders. Online viewing, which begins as harmless recreation, can become an all-consuming activity and can also lead to real sexual encounters, either with sexual partners met online or escalation of the sex addiction in general. Even when the sex involves only the computer, there is often escalation of conflict in the relationship.

> *I might say to those who say, "it's only cyber" that it's so easy to go on to more from there! I never thought the cyber addiction would be so hard to control, and I nearly went on to meet individual men myself. If I had, I think I would be dead right now because I was becoming so lackadaisical in personal protection issues.* [51-year-old woman who is herself recovering from sex addiction and is married to a sex addict]

> *It's demoralizing to have one's partner constantly focused outside the relationship for sexual stimulation and gratification. It leads to increasing dissatisfaction on the part of both parties, as the addict begins to feel that what he or she really wants sexually is "out there," and not in the relationship, and the partner feels he or she cannot get the addict's attention and affection. Destructive anger and resentment build on both sides.*

IT'S STILL CHEATING/A MENTAL AFFAIR/ADULTERY BECAUSE IT INVOLVES LYING, AND EMOTIONAL UNAVAILABILITY. Thirty respondents explained why they consider online sex activities the same as adultery. The most important reasons are listed below.

1. Having interactive sex with another person is adultery, whether or not they have skin-to-skin contact.
2. Cybersex results in lying, hiding one's activities, and covering up, and the lies are often the most painful part of an affair.

3. The spouse feels betrayed, devalued, deceived, "less than," abandoned—same as with a real affair.
4. Cybersex takes away from the sexual relationship of the couple. As one woman wrote, "I may not be getting a disease from him, but I'm not getting anything else either!"
5. A real-life person cannot compete with fantasy. The cybersex addict loses interest in his spouse because he has "ideal" relationships where there is no hassle.
6. Cybersex takes the addict away from his partner—in terms of time and emotions. It results in emotional detachment from the marriage. "I care more about what is going on in my mate's mind than any physical action!" wrote one wife.

> *The addict is using sexual energy that should be used with his wife/partner. The person on the other end of that computer is live and is participating in a sexual activity. It is one thing to masturbate to a two-dimensional image in a magazine. But to engage in an interactive sexual encounter in real time means that you are being sexual with another person. I believe that is cheating.*

> *He did have affairs, although not physically. He had affairs of the mind and that to me is as much a violation as if he actually had a physical affair with someone. Due to my religious beliefs, he committed adultery just the same as if he had another partner. Moreover, in one sense I feel that having an affair of the mind is worse than having an actual partner. My husband can, at any time, have an "affair" without leaving the house or seeing another human being.* [39-year-old woman, married 14 years]

EFFECT ON SELF-ESTEEM. The reason some respondents gave for why cybersex is so destructive is the adverse effect on their self-esteem.

> *True, you don't have the risk of the diseases, but it is still an emotional thing. It's hard to think that the sex addict wants to do it without the actual touch—how can it be better for them? Especially since they have to do all the work themselves! Plus, when the sex addict is with you, they are not really there emotionally. They are thinking about and picturing the "others" that they were with, what they were saying to them, etc. So the sex addict is getting off on something that has nothing to do with you. It really hurts your self-esteem, and most of us don't have a very good self-esteem as it is.* [37-year-old woman, married 17 years]

I CAN'T COMPETE WITH FANTASY/CAN'T MEASURE UP. Cybersex taps into partners' deepest insecurities about their ability to measure up. The need to compete with interactive sex online pressures them into unwanted sexual activities. "Sex with the fantasy leaves practically nothing left to be desired when compared with the all-too human and flawed spouse," explained one woman. Another wondered, "When he closes his eyes when we are together, what is he thinking of? The babe on the screen? Is he happy with my body? Is he grossed out?"

> *He does not have an actual human mistress from the Internet, but the Internet pornography is the "mistress" that is coming between us. The idealized images of perfect women make me feel inadequate. Conversely, the kinky and perverted behaviors shown all over the Internet fuel his beliefs and give him ammunition to say that I am the "weird one" for not wanting anal sex—"See all of the women out there on the Internet who are just crazy about it!"* [31-year-old woman, married 3 years]

On the Internet it is possible to find groups of people who are interested in all kinds of unusual or even deviant sexual practices. Interacting with these people desensitizes the user to these activities and "normalizes" them. Some cybersex users eventually come to blame their partners for being unwilling to engage in these behaviors.

IT HAS ADVERSELY AFFECTED OUR RELATIONSHIP. Some SOs focused not on the adultery aspect of cybersex, but rather on the overall effect on the couple relationship:

> *What's the fuss? I tell them that not everyone who looks at pornography is an addict, that some are merely curious. But when the addict never admits to viewing pornography, when he goes to great lengths to hide it, when he lies about his whereabouts and what he's doing, when he lies about his use of pornography to the marriage counselor he's agreed to go to because he wants to save his marriage, that's when it becomes a problem. I tell them I knew something was wrong in our intimate relationship and I always wondered who he was making love to, because it never was me.* [39-year-old woman, divorced after an 8-year marriage]

PARTNERS WHO HAVE EXPERIENCED BOTH

Several partners who had dealt with both cyberaffairs and live affairs said they hurt the same.

> *They should try it for themselves one time, and see how it feels to be less important to their partner than a picture on a computer screen! They should see what it feels like to lie in bed and know their partner is on the computer and what he is doing with it. It's not going to do much for the self-esteem. My husband has actually cheated on me and it FEELS NO DIFFERENT. The online "safe" cheating has just as dirty, filthy a feel to it as does the "real-life" cheating.* [38-year-old woman, married 18 years]

Effects on the Children

Twenty-two respondents (23.4%) reported having no children. The themes expressed by the others are shown in Table 5, in order of frequency. The

TABLE 5. Effect of Cybersex Addiction on the Children (*N* = 70)

- The kids have lost parental time and attention/lost their two-parent home. (26, 37.1%)
- The children have seen us argue, seen the stress in the home. (21, 30.0%)
- The kids are grown up and/or outside the home. (13, 18.6%)
- The children have seen pornography and/or masturbation and I'm worried for them. (10, 14.3%)
- The kids are too young to be affected/were unaffected. (9, 12.6%)
- The children have seen the pornography and have been adversely affected. (8, 11.4%)

numbers reflect how many times each theme was mentioned. Two respondents failed to answer the question, and several others expressed more than one theme, so that the total (87) is somewhat greater than 100%.

The most commonly reported adverse consequence was that one or both parents were unavailable to spend time or pay attention to the children. Respondents complained of the addict's unavailability to the children, and failure to fulfill family responsibilities: "One afternoon he was so caught up in the computer that he failed to meet my daughter coming off the school bus." "I told my husband that the only way the kids recognize him is by the back of his head." The other parent may also be unavailable because of preoccupation with the addict. SOs who got divorced or were separated mentioned that their children had lost their two-parent home.

Even if children did not see the online sexual images, they observed arguments and stress in the home; this was the second most commonly mentioned adverse effect. Two women wrote of the children witnessing episodes of domestic violence. Thirty percent of those with children believed that their young children, and adult children who were out of the home, were not significantly affected by the family problems related to online sex addiction.

Other adverse effects were related to viewing pornography (and occasionally masturbation) and to exposure to the cybersex addict's objectification of women. Some SOs reported that their children had found pornography that had been left on the computer, had walked in when the cyberaddict was chatting in a chat room, had overheard the addict having phone sex, or had observed the addict having interactive sex online. As a result, one woman wrote, "One daughter became promiscuous, the other wants me to leave him. My son now thinks that hurting women is normal." Other consequences were that the children became "horrified, ashamed, and embarrassed," got angry at the father and/or lost respect for him. Teenage children began viewing online pornography themselves. Others began selling it: "My son found old porn movies I was told had been disposed of, and he and a friend copied them and were selling them at school. My 14-year-old baby had a porn ring going!"

Several mothers were worried because their husbands surfed the Internet while supposedly watching younger children, who got to view the pornography and sometimes the masturbation.

My daughter caught him masturbating once and told me about it. I felt sick. I am scared that someday, when she gets to the age of the women that he likes to look at, that he will hurt her. I try not to dwell on this. I am also confused about how to talk to my children about love, sex, and masturbation. What do I tell my son? What do I tell my daughter? [27-year-old woman, married 3 years and still in the relationship]

WHEN BOTH PARTNERS ARE CYBERSEX USERS

There are many legitimate dating services on the Internet which have facilitated single people meeting each other. The risks and advantages of meeting in this way have been discussed before (Cooper & Sportolari, 1997). However, when two people meet online specifically for sex, then later attempt to convert the relationship to a more traditional one, there are predictable risks. A 46-year-old woman met a man online in a sexually oriented chat room. They participated in cybersex for many months, then finally met in person.

I met him online five years ago. I thought he was "faithful" to our online relationship. I found out a few months ago that he has been nonmonogamous from almost the very first time we met in person. He was into porn extensively, and into meeting "swingers." I assumed he was honest with me, but I found out otherwise. We had an amazing, exciting, and satisfying sexual relationship until he disclosed to me a few months ago. Then it turned sour. . . . I felt used and unsafe. Now he has "shelved the relationship" on his therapist's advice. I met him on online, and now I know . . . it is no different than meeting someone in 3D. People are people, and sickness and addictions are everywhere.

She reports that currently she is experiencing major depression, related to the sense of betrayal and the ending of the relationship.

Both men and women, many of them sexually compulsive, engage in online sexual activities. Not surprisingly, a sexually addicted couple can get drawn into cybersex activities. One of the survey respondents wrote that she and her husband had both been actively involved in cybersex activities with other people. Her marriage is in trouble because she is now sexually sober but her spouse is still acting out on the computer. If one member of such a couple bottoms out and seeks recovery before the other, the relationship will become destabilized.

DISCUSSION

In planning this survey, I was very concerned with issues of anonymity and privacy. It was surprising to me, therefore, that only 3 of the 94 respondents returned the survey by regular mail, thereby remaining completely anonymous. In some cases their willingness to e-mail me was situational—several commented in their survey that they were familiar with my writings. I would hypothesize that the comfort of other respondents with e-mail reflected the ease of use of the computer and sense of anonymity of the Internet culture.

Regarding sexual orientation, only two gay men and one lesbian woman responded. Cooper et al. (2000) suggest that homosexuals have different profiles in terms of online sexual acting out. However, the three partners of gay and lesbian cybersex users described very much the same dynamics, feelings, and adverse consequences as did partners of heterosexual cybersex users.

One third of respondents volunteered the information that their partner's online sexual activities had been preceded by years of other compulsive sexual behaviors. As stated earlier, the actual numbers are likely to be significantly higher. Cooper, Delmonico, and Burg (2000) reported that 4.6% of a large sample of cybersex participants were sexually compulsive, as determined by their scores on a sexual compulsivity scale. The present sample, in contrast to Cooper's cohort, was selected specifically because the cybersex use had caused significant problems for the partner. It is likely that the majority of the remaining cybersex users in the present study belonged to the "at-risk" group, those with prior vulnerability to compulsive Internet involvement.

ONLINE ADDICTION IN GENERAL VS. CYBERSEX ADDICTION

Some of the most troubling effects of a person's cybersex addiction result from the large amount of time spent on the computer. Young (1998) wrote in detail about the problems of living with a partner whose major preoccupation is computer games, making friends online, etc. Cooper et al. (1999) reported that compulsive sex use on the Internet occupies an average of 11 hours/week, time that clearly decreases the user's availability to the family. In the present study, some complaints resulted from the time element rather than from the specific content of the online material accessed:

- Partner feels lonely, ignored, unimportant, neglected, or angry because the user prefers to spend so much time on the Internet.
- Children are neglected or ignored because of the parent's involvement with the computer.

However, as this study has shown, there are additional consequences for the partner and family which result specifically from the sexual content of the user's Internet addiction:

- Many users lie repeatedly about the sexual activities; in response, their partners feel distrust and betrayal.
- The devastating emotional impact of a cybersex affair is described by many partners as similar if not the same as that of a real affair. The partner's self-esteem may be damaged; strong feelings of hurt, betrayal, abandon-

ment, devastation, loneliness, shame, isolation, humiliation, and jealousy are evoked.

- The couple's sexual relationship suffers, not only generally because the user stays up much of the night, but specifically because the spouse (and often the user) compares her body and her sexual performance to that of the online women and believes she can't measure up.
- Online sexual activities may be followed by physical contact with others; the partner may retaliate or seek solace in extramarital affairs.
- Children may be exposed to pornography and may develop unhealthy attitudes toward sex and women.

Divorce and separation were two other consequences of cybersex addiction which were common in this survey. We may speculate that more couples get divorced over cybersex addiction than over excessive time spent on the Internet in general. Also, it is probable that workers who use company time to access the Internet are more likely to get fired if the content of their Internet activity was sexual than if it was not.

THE STAGES OF PRERECOVERY OF THE CYBERSEX COADDICT

In this study, SOs were aware of the cybersex addict's online activities for time periods ranging from eight years to just a month or two. It is possible to infer from the survey responses the time course of responses by the partner to the cyberaddict's ongoing involvement with online sex.

STAGE 1: IGNORANCE/DENIAL

The partner recognizes there is a problem in the relationship but is unaware of the contribution of cybersex to the problem. ("I knew something was wrong the first two years of our marriage, but I could not identify it.") The SO believes the addict's denials, explanations, and promises. She tends to ignore and explain away her own concerns, and may blame herself for the sexual problems. When cybersex addiction is present, a frequent problem is lack of interest by the addict in marital sex; in response the SO may try to enhance her own attractiveness to the addict. Self-esteem is likely to suffer, but the partner is unlikely to seek help at this point.

Late in this stage, suspicions may increase and "detective behaviors" begin. However, snooping or detective behaviors are accentuated at a later stage.

STAGE 2: SHOCK/DISCOVERY OF THE CYBERSEX ACTIVITIES

At some point the partner learns of the cybersex addict's activities. In some cases this occurs accidentally, either because the partner comes upon the addict in the midst of the activities, or because the SO turns on the computer and discovers a cache of pornographic pictures. In other cases, the discovery is the result of deliberate investigations by the SO. No matter how the discovery occurs, the result is that the partner's ignorance and denial are over.

Discovery often leads to strong emotions of shock, betrayal, anger, pain, hopelessness, confusion, and shame. Because the pull of the computer is so strong and its availability in the home and at work is so great, there is a great tendency for the addict to return to cybersex activities even after discovery by the spouse, no matter how sincere the initial intention to quit. The result is that many respondents described a cycle of discoveries, promises made and broken, and additional discoveries and promises.

> *I took my engagement ring off several times, each time I found out about his online activities—and each time I believed his promises not to do it again. I coped by blaming myself, by not looking too closely at it. I thought because he admitted he had a problem that things would get better, but he was still in denial. I am coping better with it now that I am not in the relationship.* [29-year-old woman who eventually ended her engagement]

ISOLATION

Feelings of shame, self-blame, and embarrassment often accompany the early days of dealing with a partner's cybersex addiction. These feelings may prevent the SO from talking with others and appealing for help, and the resultant isolation worsens the situation. Covering up for the addict is part of this stage.

> *We have only told our therapists about this problem. It's so hard to go to family events and everyone thinks we're doing great. I don't want to tell them because I don't want this to be all that they think of when they think of my husband. And we don't feel like we can trust any of our friends with our "secret." So we're dealing with this alone and that hurts.* [25-year-old woman, married 2 years, just recently discovered the cybersex addiction]

> *I was in counseling for codependency issues, but I couldn't bring myself to tell the counselor what the real problem was, I was so embarrassed.* [33-year-old woman, married 11 years, dealing with cyberporn for 2 years]

STAGE 3: PROBLEM-SOLVING ATTEMPTS

The partner is now energized to take action to resolve the problem, which is perceived as the cybersex behaviors. At this stage the classic sexual coaddictive behaviors peak—snooping, bargaining, controlling access to the computer, giving ultimatums, asking for full disclosure after every episode, obtaining information for the addict on sex addiction and addiction recovery, and (early in this stage) increasing the frequency and repertory of sexual activities with the addict in hopes of decreasing his desire for cybersex.

> *The breaking point became his willingness to lie to me to cover his activities and his shame. We both knew this would not work and I especially would spiral downhill when I would find out he had broken his promises. At some*

point I had asked that if he acted out that he tell me right away so that we could work with it. My preference of course was that he come to me when he felt like acting out, but that didn't happen. I could deal with the addiction if it were out in the open, because we would both begin to gain insights into the why's of this complicated issue. [38-year-old woman, married 8 years]

This type of agreement rarely works for long. It provides a measure of comfort for the wife to know what is going on and gives her the illusion of control. But the result establishes a parent–child dynamic between the couple, engenders resentment in the addict, and typically ends up in continued lying.

I was angry, hurt, offended, I couldn't trust him. I would try to control his behavior, I would sneak around to see if he had accessed the Internet without me knowing, I would try to delete his files, cancel the Internet, plead with him to stop, you name it. [26-year-old woman, separating after a 4-year marriage]

A sexual solution to the sexual problem seems to make sense in this stage. SOs may agree to sexual practices with which they are not comfortable, have sex even when tired, and think about improving their appearance by undergoing breast enhancement surgery or liposuction. For the cybersex user, none of these methods are likely to diminish the lure of the Internet.

The partner believes that additional information will enhance her or his ability to manage the situation. This leads to "snooping" or "detective" behaviors. Coaddicts who are computer savvy learn how to trace the addict's activities, and in some cases may even try to entice him by logging on into the same chat rooms themselves.

I found myself making up screen names to get him to chat with me to see how far he goes with his cybersex. I have also answered his personal ads with made-up information, only to find him asking for my phone number. I also keep my screen name blocked and at times (when I wasn't with him at night) I would log on the computer at 2 or 3 AM only to find him online in a chat room. I have also logged on to his computer to check what areas he had visited, what new pictures he had downloaded. [35-year-old woman who found out about the cybersex 6 months earlier]

CONTRACTS ABOUT COMPUTER AND CYBERSEX ACTIVITIES

When the cybersex activities come to light, the couple tries to come to some agreement to try to limit the addict's use of the computer. This may consist simply of promises not to use it, or to restrict usage to legitimate needs. Often, the SO, with the addict's agreement or at least knowledge, assumes control of the access. In addition, the SO or the couple may purchase filtering software (e.g., Net Nanny) which prevents access to sexually oriented sites. None of these "negative" methods tend to be successful for long if they are not accompanied by "positive" recovery-oriented activities.

I have spied on his e-mail. I am computer proficient and he is not. I have deleted his screen name when he could not handle the smorgasbord of women online, as he puts it. I am in control of the parental controls on AOL and when I gave him a screen name back, I have him locked out of chat rooms and have his instant message access restricted to certain people. This prevents his anonymous cruising. [47-year-old woman, married 30 years]

The above three stages—ignorance/denial, shock/discovery of the cybersex, and problem-solving attempts—are specific applications of the phases of prerecovery of sexual coaddicts described by Milrad (1999). She found that the prerecovery stage, lasting approximately 4–8 years, was divided into two phases—a denial phase, when partners recognize there is a problem but remain in denial about its cause, and a more active phase, when they come out of denial about the addict's problem and seek active solutions, but remain in denial as to their own issues.

The findings of this survey support Milrad's phases. As she observed in her study, the end of the prerecovery phase and the beginning of recovery is an awareness by sexual coaddicts that they are in crisis and need help. In the present study, SOs entered the crisis stage when they realized that their problem-solving efforts were unsuccessful and when the costs of remaining in the status quo became intolerable—depressive symptoms, isolation, loss of libido, a "dead" marriage, their own dysfunctional behaviors in some cases (affairs, excessive drinking, violence), and awareness of the effects on the children of the family dysfunction. This is the stage when the SO seeks help for herself/himself rather than in order to fix the addict, and learns that she/he did not cause the problem and cannot solve it. Once the SO is in therapy and getting help, the chances increase that the marriage or relationship will end unless the cybersex addict too becomes committed to recovery.

SEXUAL ANOREXIA AND CYBERSEX ADDICTION

The concept of sexual anorexia, essentially a synonym for sexual aversion disorder (DSM-IV, 1994, p. 499), has been presented as part of the continuum of addictive sexual disorders. Patrick Carnes (1997, p. 1) defined sexual anorexia as "an obsessive state in which the physical, mental, and emotional task of avoiding sex dominates one's life." Sexual anorexia is analogous to food anorexia, a disorder in which food occupies an obsessive place in the person's psyche, but the goal is to avoid it. Food, or sex, becomes the enemy, to be feared and avoided.

The concept of sexual anorexia is a very valuable one, but it is often misused and misunderstood when a person is labeled sexually anorexic because he does not engage in sex in one particular context (e.g., within the couple relationship). More than one SO reported that a therapist or counselor, after hearing about the lack of relational sex between the two, had labeled the cybersex addict "anorexic." Cybersex addicts do not avoid sex; on the contrary, they are sexually compulsive. However, they often redirect their sexual interest away from the SO and toward the computer. A therapist who does not ask the right questions, or is lied to by the addict, may assume that no couple sex is the same as no sex at all. The lesson to be learned here is that it is crucial for the therapist to get a thorough sexual history, and, especially, to inquire at length about the presence of online sexual activity in the life of a client who appears not to be interested in sex with the partner. The lesson for SOs is that repeated statements such as "I'm too tired, I've been working too hard," "I just have a low libido," "If you were sexier . . . " may indeed represent sexual anorexia, but they may instead be a sign that the person is too involved with other sexual activities.

IMPLICATIONS FOR THERAPISTS

In my survey, several people consulted counselors who apparently failed to obtain an adequate history and therefore missed the diagnosis. Some counselors urged the SO to initiate sex more frequently. Some had never heard of sexual addiction or compulsivity. Others were so committed to being nonjudgmental that they missed the big picture.

> *It scared me that my fiance went to Internet sites to see young girls [aged 14 and up]. I talked with my pastor about it and he told me he thought it was just curiosity, that once we were married, my husband's curiosity would be filled by me. Now that we are married, I find that he has continued his acting out and lied to me so much that I am afraid of what could happen if we have children and one is a girl.* [29-year-old woman, newly married]

A client's complaints about her spouse's cybersex use may simply reflect her own discomfort with pornography, or else may be a sign of a significant cybersex addiction problem in the family; each of these requires a different treatment approach. Where sexual compulsivity is in fact present, potential mistakes by the uninformed counselor are

- to underestimate the adverse consequences of the behavior,
- to diagnose the couple's problem as poor communication or a need by the SO of greater acceptance of the Internet user's activities,
- to diagnose the addict's problem as sexual anorexia, and
- to recommend that the cybersex user limit the time devoted to cybersex activities to some predetermined number of hours (rather than stopping altogether), or to have the SO join in the addict's cybersex activities.

The first step for the counselor is to gather information, preferably from both partners. Ask specific questions:

- What is a typical day in the life of each partner, hour by hour?
- Are there large chunks of time that are unaccounted for?

- Have there been changes in the couple's sexual relationship? In the amount of time the family spends together? In the time spent with children?
- Is there evidence of cybersex involvement?
- Is there a history of other compulsive sexual behaviors?

Ask about the SO's beliefs regarding sex, pornography, and masturbation. Obtain a thorough sexual history from both partners, and a history of their sexual relationship with each other.

If cybersex addiction is indeed present, the basic principles are the same as with any form of sex addiction: Initially, the addict needs to be helped to break through the denial that a problem exists and to recognize the impact of the behaviors on the partner and family; to stop the behaviors and associated lying; to stop blaming the SO; to learn problem solving in ways other than escape through cybersex activities; and to develop strategies for dealing with sexual urges. Support through membership in 12-step programs such as Sex Addicts Anonymous (SAA), Sexaholics Anonymous (SA), or Sex and Love Addicts Anonymous (SLAA) is as useful as with any other addiction. Strategies specific to the computer include

- moving the computer to an open area
- not using the Internet
- using the computer only for specific, planned tasks
- being online only when family members are around
- adding net safety tools and screens
- arranging for some accountability regarding Internet access at work.

Such strategies are discussed in greater detail in the other articles in this issue of the journal.

For the spouse or SO, the negative consequences detailed in this article constitute a lengthy list of issues to explore in therapy. Although the presence of the computer in the home gives the problem an immediacy and visibility which are absent when the addiction can be better hidden, counseling is basically the same as with any other form of addiction. Early on, the SO needs validation of her belief that a real problem does exist, and of her perception that cybersex addiction can be as damaging to the relationship as more traditional sexual affairs. She needs to feel "heard" by the counselor, and encouraged to state her needs. Other early goals of therapy are to help the client accept that (s)he did not cause the problem, cannot control it, and cannot cure it, and that belief that having enough information will allow control of the situation is an illusion. The focus needs to be moved from fixing the other person to working on oneself, especially one's damaged self-esteem, and learning to pay attention to one's own needs and desires. Education about appropriate boundaries is useful, along with development of appropriate boundaries regarding the presence of the computer in the home and conditions for its use. Except perhaps very temporarily, however, it is not generally useful to have the SO be the "keeper" of the computer or to control the cybersex addict's access; this is better left to the addict's therapist or sponsor. Like the cybersex addict, the SO can be greatly helped and supported by membership in a 12-step program such as S-Anon, COSA, or Al-Anon.

LIMITATIONS OF THIS STUDY

The chief limitation of this study is that it includes only a self-selected population of people who have experienced significant adverse consequences as a result of their partner's cybersex addiction. It can provide no information about (a) the nature of the consequences, if any, to families of recreational or occasional cybersex users or (b) the prevalence among all cybersex users of significant consequences to the family. A random sample of partners of all cybersex users would be needed to provide such information.

Conclusions

The present study was based on a brief survey completed by 91 women and 3 men who believed they had experienced serious adverse consequences resulting from their significant other's cybersex addiction. In 60.6% of cases the sexual activities were limited to cybersex and did not include offline sex. Although not specifically asked about this, 31% of partners volunteered that the cybersex activities were a continuation of preexisting compulsive sexual behaviors. Open-ended questions yielded the following conclusions.

1. In response to learning about the partner's online sexual activities, the survey respondents experienced strong feelings of hurt, betrayal, rejection, abandonment, devastation, loneliness, shame, isolation, humiliation, jealousy, and anger, as well as loss of self-esteem. Being lied to repeatedly was a major cause of distress for the respondents.
2. Cybersex addiction was a major contributing factor to separation and divorce of couples in this survey: 22.3% of the respondents were no longer living with the cybersex addict, and several others were seriously contemplating leaving.
3. Among 68% of the couples one or both of the pair had lost interest in relational sex; only 32% of respondents did not report an adverse effect on the couple's sexual relationship. Partners related that 52.1% of the addicts had decreased interest in sex with their primary partner, as did 34% of the partners. Some couples had had no relational sex in months or years. Partners and therapists sometimes labeled these addicts as "sexually anorexic," but in fact they were very active sexually—but with the computer rather than with their spouses.
4. Partners tended to compare themselves unfavorably with the online women

and pictures, and to feel hopeless about being able to compete with them.

5. Partners overwhelmingly reported feeling that cyberaffairs were as emotionally painful to them as live or offline affairs and that virtual affairs were just as much adultery or "cheating" as live affairs; this was equally true of partners who had experience of their cybersex addicts having both types of affairs. Cybersex activities were considered particularly destructive in that they (a) took place right in the home and (b) were so time consuming.

6. Adverse effects on the children of cybersex addicts included (a) exposure of children to cyberporn and to objectification of women, (b) involvement of the children in the conflict between the parents, (c) lack of attention to the children because of one parent's involvement with the computer and the other parent's preoccupation with the cybersex addict, and (d) breakup of the marriage.

7. In response to their spouses' cybersex addiction, partners went through a sequence of prerecovery phases which consisted of (a) ignorance/denial, (b) shock/discovery of cybersex activities, and (c) problem-solving attempts. When their attempts failed and they realized how unmanageable their lives had become, they entered the crisis stage and began their own recovery.

REFERENCES

American Psychiatric Association. (1994). *Diagnostic and statistical manual of mental disorders, 4th Edition.* Washington, DC: American Psychiatric Association.

Carnes, P. J., with Moriarity, J. M. (1997). *Sexual anorexia.* Center City, MN: Hazelden.

Carnes, P. J. (1991). *Don't call it love.* New York: Bantam Books.

Computerworld. (1998). *Commerce by numbers—Internet population* [Online]. Available: http://www.computerworld.com/home/Emmerce.nsf/All/pop

Cooper, A., Delmonico, D. L., & Burg, R. (2000). Cybersex users, abusers, and compulsives: New findings and implications. *Sexual Addiction & Compulsivity, 7,* 5–29.

Cooper, A., Putnam, D. A., Planchon, L. A., & Boies, S. C. (1999). Online sexual compulsivity: Getting tangled in the Net. *Sexual Addiction & Compulsivity, 6,* 79-104.

Cooper, A., & Sportolari, L. (1997). Romance in cyberspace: Understanding online attraction. *Journal of Sex Education and Therapy, 22,* 71–74.

Milrad, R., (1999). Coaddictive recovery: Early recovery issues for spouses of sex addicts. *Sexual Addiction & Compulsivity, 6,* 125–136.

Schneider, J. P., Corley, M. D., & Irons, R. R., (1998). Surviving disclosure of infidelity: Results of an international survey of 164 recovering sex addicts and partners. *Sexual Addiction & Compulsivity, 5,* 189–218.

Schneider, J. P., & Schneider, B. H. (1990). *Sex, lies, and forgiveness: Couples speaking on healing from sex addiction.* Center City, MN: Hazelden Educational Materials.

Schneider, J. P. & Schneider, B. H. (1996). Couple recovery from sexual addiction/ coaddiction: Results of a survey of 88 marriages. *Sexual Addiction & Compulsivity, 3,* 111–126.

Young, K. S. (1998). *Caught in the Net.* New York: John Wiley & Sons

Chapter 3

Online Infidelity: A New Dimension in Couple Relationships with Implications for Evaluation and Treatment

KIMBERLY S. YOUNG
Center for Online Addiction, Bradford, Pennsylvania, USA

ERIC GRIFFIN-SHELLEY
Private Practice, Lafayette Hill, Pennsylvania, USA

AL COOPER
Stanford University, Stanford, California, USA

JAMES O'MARA and JENNIFER BUCHANAN
University of Pittsburgh, Pittsburgh, Pennsylvania, USA

Prior research has examined how Internet addiction can impact couple relationships. This article investigates how with the advent of the Internet a new dimension has been created for romantic and sexual relationships. Reports are suggesting that electronic communication can lead to marital discord, separation, and possible divorce. The ACE model (Anonymity, Convenience, Escape), which was hypothesized as a driving force behind cybersexual addiction, provides a framework to explain the underlying cyber-cultural dynamics that can increase the risk of virtual adultery. Warning signs of a cyberaffair are outlined to alert clients and therapists to this new aspect of couple relationships. Clinicians working in the aftermath of an online romantic and/or sexual encounter need to improve a couple's communication and cohesion and to assess for more severe problems such as sexual addiction. Specific interventions focus on strategies for rebuilding trust, ways to improve marital communication, educating couples on whether these behaviors indicate an underlying addictive process, and how to restore trust and commitment after a cyberaffair.

Address correspondence to Dr. Kimberly S. Young, Executve Director, Center for On-Line Addiction, P.O. Box 72, Bradford, PA 16701, USA. Web site: http://netaddiction.com

INTRODUCTION

Recent research has explored the existence and extent of pathological Internet use (Brenner, 1997; Cooper, 1998a, Cooper, Putnam, Planchon, & Boies, 1999; Cooper, Scherer, Boies, & Gordon, 1999; Griffiths, 1996, 1997; Morahan-Martin, 1997; Scherer, 1997; Young, 1997a, 1997b, 1998a, 1998b) and its significant impact on social, academic, and occupational roles. More important, this research (Griffiths, 1997; Young, 1998a, 1998b, 1999a) and prior research on computer addiction (Shotton, 1991) has observed that computer and/or Internet-dependent users gradually spent less time with real people in their lives in exchange for solitary time in front of a computer and online relationships. Young (1998a) found that serious relationship problems were reported by 53% of the 396 case studies of Internet addicts interviewed, with marriages and intimate dating relationships most disrupted due to cyberaffairs and online sexual compulsivity. In their study Cooper, Scherer et al. (1999) found that over 8% manifested signs of sexual compulsivity, 32% acknowledged that their online sexual pursuits had interfered with one important dimension of their lives, and 22% that their online sexual pursuits had actually jeopardized at least one of these important dimensions.

A cyberaffair is defined as a romantic and/or sexual relationship that is initiated via online contact and maintained predominantly through electronic conversations that occur through e-mail and in virtual communities such as chat rooms, interactive games, or newsgroups (Young, 1999a). Virtual or online communities allow strangers from all over the world to meet instantly 24 hours per day, seven days a week.

There are a number of factors that make online contacts dynamically different and potentially seductive. First, given the global nature of the Internet, online relationships can be culturally diverse and consequently can seem more glamorous than the people one already knows in day-to-day living (Young, 1997a). Second, electronic communication apparently allows at least some individuals to subjectively feel less inhibited. Consequently, in the expression of their emotions, people are more likely to be open, honest, and forthright in revealing personal truths. As a result, the appearance of intimacy that might take months or years in an offline relationship may only take days or weeks online. This perceived sense of trust, intimacy, and acceptance has the potential to encourage online users to use these relationships as a primary source of companionship and comfort (Cooper & Sportolari, 1997; Young, 1997a).

Furthermore, once the person has begun to use online relationships to get their needs met, such online comfort can easily turn into mutual erotic dialogue, often known as "cybersex." Cybersex involves two online users engaging in private discourse about sexual fantasies. The dialogue is typically accompanied by sexual self-stimulation (Young, 1997a). Emotional intimacy can lead to cybersex, and the reverse is also possible. Cooper, Putnam, et al. (1999) offer three types of users (recreational, "at risk," and compulsive) who engage in online sexual pursuits, any of which has the potential to find themselves involved in a cyberaffair.

Compulsivity with general computer use may create the framework for escalating time online. In addition those with sexually compulsive features may find the Internet to be an attractive venue in which to pursue these interests. For some, time online can quickly progress into talking with a "cyberlover" and/or various forms of cybersex. For some an online relationship will progress into secret phone calls, letters, and offline meetings. Others prefer the distance and relative anonymity and control offered by the Internet and will prefer to confine the relationship to cyberspace. In either case, getting one's needs met through a cyberaffair will adversely impact an ongoing, long-term, face-to-face relationship and is likely to cause marital discord, separation, and can even contribute to divorce (Young, 1998a, 1999a). Clinicians are increasingly seeing evidence of this as clients present with concerns about how this new form of infidelity, the virtual affair, is impacting their relationships and thus need to be aware of this trend as they assess couples and plan treatment strategies.

Online infidelity has accounted for a growing number of divorce cases according to the President of the American Academy of Matrimonial Lawyers (Quittner, 1997). However, the nature and scope of marital dissolution caused by such virtual infidelity may have been underestimated due to the Internet's current popularity as a technological advancement (Young, 1999a). Furthermore, health care professionals, especially marital and family therapists who are most likely to intervene and treat these couples in crisis, are too often unfamiliar with the dynamics associated with relatively new concepts of cyberaffairs and cybersex.

Young's ACE model (Anonymity, Convenience, Escape) was developed to explain cybersexual addiction (1999b) and is a variant of Cooper's (1998a) Triple-A Engine (Access, Affordability, and Anonymity) which was offered to help understand the power and attraction of the Internet for sexual pursuits. In this article the ACE model will be used as a framework to clarify the underlying motivation of online infidelity and to outline specific treatment strategies in working with couples dealing with these issues.

POTENTIAL EXPLANATIONS OF INFIDELITY ONLINE

Imagine a husband, who would never walk into an adult bookstore, finding that he could download online pornography cheaply, quickly, and without detection. Picture a wife, who would never pick up the telephone to dial a 900 number, who discovers almost by chance that she can engage in erotic chat or phone sex with men she met online apparently free of observation. Seemingly stable long-term relationships have never been faced with the challenge of private, inexpensive, and easily accessible cybersex and/or cyberaffairs. These scenarios are suddenly plaguing couples today and neither they nor their counselors are adequately prepared to deal with this new potential temptation.

In order to understand the increased incidence of sex and infidelity online, the ACE model was developed to explain how cyberspace creates a cultural climate of permissiveness that actually serves to encourage and validate sexually adulterous and promiscuous online behavior (Young, 1999b). The ACE model proposes three variables (anonymity, convenience, and escape) that can lead to virtual adultery.

Anonymity

First, the anonymity of electronic transactions allows users to secretly engage in erotic chats without the fear of being caught by a spouse. This anonymity also provides the user with a greater sense of perceived control over the content, tone, and nature of the online experience. Online experiences often occur in the privacy of one's home, office, or bedroom, facilitating the perception of anonymity and that Internet use is personal and untraceable. Cyberaffairs initiated via online communication (Young, 1999a) typically begin in chat room settings which allow users to talk in real time by typing messages to each other using "screen names" or "handles." Messages can either appear in the public forum for the entire room to read or a more personal e-mail or "instant message" can be sent privately to a single member of the room.

The anonymity associated with electronic communication and general milieu of the Internet often facilitates more open and frank communication with other users (Cooper & Sportolari, 1997). Anonymity can also increase the online user's feeling of comfort since there is a decreased ability to look for, and thus detect, signs of insincerity, disapproval, or judgment in facial expression, as would be typical in face-to-face interactions. The distance afforded by cyberspace enables a person to share intimate feelings often reserved for a significant other thus opening the door for bonding and an accelerated sense of intimacy, which in turn can evolve into a cyberaffair or cybersex.

Convenience

Next, the convenience of interactive online applications such as e-mail, ICQ (a popular online interaction program which stands for "I seek you"), chat rooms, newsgroups, or role-playing games provide a vehicle to meet others. The proliferation of special interest rooms, groups, and games contributes to easy access for a curious person's initial exploration. Most people do not yet realize that there is any risk involved in engaging in online sexual pursuits. Sex is the number one searched topic (Cooper, Scherer, et al., 1999) and as many as one third of all Internet users visit some type of sexual site (Cooper, Delmonico, & Burg, 2000).

While in some ways it may seem like a journey into "foreign territory," online sexual behaviors occur in the familiar and comfortable environment of home or office thus reducing the feeling of risk and allowing even more adventurous behaviors. What starts off as a simple e-mail exchange or an innocent chat room encounter can escalate into an intense and passionate cyberaffair and eventually into face-to-face sexual encounters. A curious person may be completely unprepared when they step into one of many rooms specifically designed for the purposes of facilitating infidelity. Titles such as the MarriedM4Affair, Cheating Wife, or Lonely Husband may intrigue a casual browser who is initially shocked, but at the same time titillated by the permissiveness of others engaged in virtual adultery. Such virtual environments are more seductive than most people anticipate and clearly can lead down a path providing short-term comfort, distraction, and/or excitement. However, in most cases, the virtual relationships are short lived. Nonetheless, involvement in cybersex and/or cyberaffairs ultimately exacerbates face-to-face relational problems and can damage if not destroy the relationship (Young, 1998a).

Escape

A husband who lives in New York considers it "harmless" to flirt with a woman who lives in Australia because, prior to surfing cyberspace, physical distance meant that nothing would actually happen between the people involved. A wife can rationalize that having cybersex isn't really infidelity because, in the past, the lack of physical contact meant that such fantasies, like her fantasies about movie stars, would never be realized. However, once unleashed, the power of a cyberaffair and/or cybersex can lead a once open and loving man to become evasive and to demand his privacy online. This "new frontier" in relationship dynamics can lead a once warm and compassionate wife and mother to turn to the computer and its cyberworld lovers and/or sex partners and away from caring for her children. Partially as a result of the general population and health care professionals not yet being attuned to the risks, seemingly "harmless" cyberromps can result in serious difficulties way beyond what was expected or intended. When a spouse leaves a long-term and apparently stable marriage for the allure of someone they recently met over the Internet, it illustrates the power and allure of the myriad of online sexual and/or romantic possibilities (Young, 1998a).

People may mistakenly assume that the primary reinforcement to engage in an online affair or virtual adultery is the sexual gratification enjoyed by the participants. However, there may be more to these behaviors than simple reinforcement. So-called "process" or "behavioral" addictions do not require the ingestion of chemicals that are necessary to produce the physiological dependence characteristic of chemical dependency, e.g., to drugs, alcohol, or cigarettes. People become addicted to sex, money, gambling, and the Internet through a process that creates at least a psychological dependence if not a physiological dependency on chemicals. Some theorists, e.g., Milkman and Sunderwirth (1987), believe that behavioral addictions rely on the manipulation of endogenous chemicals found in the brain. Online sexual compulsivity and Internet affairs can develop into addictive behaviors, involving neurochemical reinforcement. These online sexual compulsives and Internet addicts rationalize and defend behaviors that appear, at least to others, to have high risk and significantly negative consequences.

The experience of an online affair, with or without a sexual component, may be reinforced through a type of drug or neurochemical "high." The pursuit of a "high" is characteristic of addictions (Griffin-Shelley, 1991). The "high" provides an emotional or mental escape and serves to reinforce the behavior. Excessive involvement in this escapist activity can lead to compulsivity or addiction (Young, 1997a, 1998a, 1998b). A lonely wife in an empty marriage can escape into a chat room where she is desired by her many cyberpartners. A sexually insecure husband can transform into a hot cyberlover whom all the women in the chat room fight over. While sexual fulfillment may provide either the initial or subsequent reinforcement, the more potent reinforcement is the ability to cultivate a subjective fantasy world. Online romantic and/or sexual behavior can provide a potent escape from the stresses and strains of real life. These activities fall on what Cooper, Putnam et al. (1999) describe as a continuum from life enhancing to pathological and addictive. Clearly, escapist fantasies can become pathological and addictive.

Evidence for the power of online addiction is mounting in a variety of settings. While empirical validation is just starting to be published (Cooper et al., 2000; Cooper, Scherer et al., 1999) and widely recognized, the courts have already argued the role of online compulsivity as a mental disorder in the defense of online sexual deviancy cases. For example, one landmark case, the United States versus McBroom, successfully demonstrated that the client's downloading, viewing, and transferring of Internet pornography was less about erotic gratification and more about an emotional escape mechanism to relieve mental tension. Until further research has been accumulated, preliminary evidence such as the above and the increasingly common clinical presentation of cyberaffairs and cybercompulsions in treatment rooms will have to point the way toward serious consideration of these problems for marital relationships.

IMPLICATIONS FOR MARITAL THERAPY

While the ACE model (of cybersexual addiction) provides a framework to understand the cyberspace climate that often serves to encourage the initiation of a cyberaffair, clinicians working in the aftermath of such cases need guidance on appropriate ways to assess the severity of the problem and to help the couples involved. This section outlines specific interventions that may help counsel couples, identify the nature of the problem, improve inter-personal communication between the partners, and rebuild trust so that con-tinued commitment is possible after the discovery of cybersex and/or a cyberaffair.

Detection of a Suspected Cyberaffair

Unlike spouses who catch their partners in real-life adultery, spouses may enter counseling with little more than a suspicion that their partner is sharing intimacies with someone via the computer. As with face-to-face infidelity, the first step is to evaluate the situation. These early warning signs can be a guide to both clients and therapists.

CHANGE IN SLEEP PATTERNS. Chat rooms and meeting places for cybersex don't heat up until late at night, so the unfaithful partner may tend to stay up later and later to be part of the "action." A partner may begin to come to bed in the early morning hours or they may leap out of bed an hour or two early to use the computer for a prework e-mail exchange with a new romantic partner.

A DEMAND FOR PRIVACY. Cooper, Scherer, et al. (1999) found that almost 70% of their sample kept secret the amount of time they went online for sexual pursuits. Significantly more men (72%) then women (62%) report keeping this a secret. If someone begins an affair, whether online or offline, he usually goes to great lengths to hide the truth from his partner. With a cyberaffair, this attempt usually leads to the need for greater privacy and secrecy sur-rounding their computer usage. The computer may be moved from the visible den to a secluded corner of a locked study, or one person may change the password or cloak all their online activities in secrecy. If disturbed or inter-rupted when online, they may react with anger or defensiveness (Young, 1999a).

OTHER RESPONSIBILITIES IGNORED. When any Internet user increases his time online, other responsibilities often suffer (Young, 1998a). This is not automatically a sign of a cyberaffair, but in a relationship, those dirty dishes, piles of laun-dry, increased time at the office, and unmowed lawns might indicate that someone else is competing for the suspected person's attention and time. At the same time with the excitement and novelty of being involved in an online affair the person may not feel as much motivation to contribute to the other responsibilities in which they may have formerly felt more invested.

EVIDENCE OF LYING. The offending spouse may hide credit card bills for online services and telephone bills to calls made to a cyberlover and lie about the reason for such extensive Internet use (Young, 1998a). As noted earlier most people will lie about their online sexual behaviors, but those engaging in a cyberaffair have a higher stake in concealing the truth. This often triggers bigger and bolder lies—including telling a spouse that they will quit or cut back their Internet usage. It is important to remember that frequent attempts to decrease or discontinue sexual behaviors is one of the indications of sexual compulsivity (Griffin-Shelley, 1991; Cooper, 1998b).

PERSONALITY CHANGES. A person is often surprised and confused to see how much their partner's moods and behaviors have changed since the Internet engulfed them. A once warm and sensitive wife becomes cold and withdrawn. A formerly jovial husband turns quiet and brooding (Young, 1998a). If questioned about these changes in connection with their Internet activities, the person engaging in a cyberaffair often responds with heated denials, blaming, and rationalization. The motivation, either consciously or not, is to shift the blame to the nonoffending partner. For a person once willing to communicate about contentious matters, this could be a smokescreen hiding a cyberaffair.

LOSS OF INTEREST IN SEX. Some cyberaffairs evolve into phone sex or an actual rendezvous, but cybersex alone often includes mutual masturbation from the confines of each person's computer room. When a person suddenly shows a lesser interest in sex, it may be an indicator that they have found another sexual outlet. If sexual activity continues, the unfaithful partner is likely to be less enthusiastic, energetic, and responsive to lovemaking as it is difficult for any ongoing sexual relationship to compete with the newness and excitement of a new partner (Young, 1998a).

DECLINING INVESTMENT IN THE RELATIONSHIP. Those engaged in a cyberaffair are likely to have less energy to participate in the relationship in any number of ways. They shun those familiar rituals like a shared bath, talking over the dishes after dinner, or renting a video on Saturday night. They don't get as excited about taking vacations together and they avoid talk about long-range plans. As they are having their fun with someone else, their thoughts and energies revolve around fantasies of their cyberpartner—not building intimacy with the long-term partner.

In addition to identifying warning signs, clients and therapists may need instruments and interventions to assess the type and severity of the problem. Are they dealing with a onetime virtual liaison, an ongoing cyberaffair, sexual addiction, codependency, relationship dependency, and/or online sexual addiction? Screening questionnaires for several of these problems have been developed including cybersexual addiction, sex addiction, 12-step recovery, and relationship dependency.

Additional interventions could include bibliotherapy where clients read relevant books (e.g., *Sex, Lies, and Forgiveness* by Schneider and Schneider, 1999) and attendance at 12-step fellowship meetings. Couples can share

Professionally Developed Screens:
1. Cybersexual Addiction Test:
   http://www.netaddiction.com/cybersexual_addiction.htm
2. Online Sexual Addiction Questionnnaire (OSA-Q) by Dana Putnam:
   http://www.onlinesexaddict.com/osaq.html
3. Male Sexual Addiction Screening Test (S.A.S.T.) by Patrick Carnes, Ph.D. and Robert Weiss, L.C.S.W.: http://www.sexhelp.com
4. Women's Sexual Screening Addiction Test by Patrick Carnes Ph.D. and Sharon O'Hara, M.A.: http://www.sexhelp.com
5. Sexaholics Anonymous (S.A.) Test: http://www.sa.org
6. Sexual Compulsives Anonymous (S.C.A.): http://www.sca- recovery.org
7. Sex Addicts Anonymous (S.A.A.): http://www.sexaa.org
8. Sexual Recovery Anonymous (S.R.A.): http://ourworld.compuserve.com/ homepages/sra/
9. Sexual Codependency Sexual Coaddiction Questionnaire by Jennifer Schneider, M.D.: http://www.azstarnet.com/~jschndr
10. The S-Anon Checklist: http://www.sanon.org/
11. COSA: Key Identifying Behaviors: http://www.shore.net/~cosa

with each other or with their therapist their reactions, thoughts, and feelings regarding any of these activities.

Improving Interpersonal Communication

The discovery of an unfaithful partner is difficult for any person to accept. People can react to an Internet affair with doubt, jealousy toward the computer or the Internet, and a fear that the relationship will end because of someone a partner has yet to meet in "real life." Reactions vary but often partners initially become enablers as they rationalize their partner's behavior as just a "phase." Often they will also go to great lengths to conceal the problem from family and friends (Young, 1999a).

In addition to enabling behaviors, some partners have more serious problems, i.e., their own codependency (Schneider, 1988; Milrad, 1999). Their deep fears of abandonment and/or their histories of abuse may have created their own relationship dependency issues that disempower them from dealing directly with the violation.

The effort to conceal a cyberaffair coupled with a partner's rationalization of the marital problem often impairs the couple's ability to communicate truthfully. Therefore, when working directly with the couple, practitioners should assist them in basic communication skills to improve open, effective, and honest communication without blame or anger. Some general guidelines follow.

SET SPECIFIC GOALS. Parameters should be established in terms of the communication goals within the counseling session. To facilitate goal setting, a clinician should pose such questions as, "Do you both want to save the relationship?", "Have you ended the cyberaffair, or are you prepared to?", "Are there indications of other forms of Internet or non-Internet sexual acting out?", "What are each of your expectations about future online sexual pursuits?", and "What is needed to rebuild trust in the relationship and what first step is each of you prepared to make?" These goal-setting questions evaluate a couple's expectations related to sexuality and Internet usage and assess their commitment and desire to rebuild the present relationship.

USE NONJUDGMENTAL LANGUAGE. Particularly in these highly charged and emotional situations, clinicians need to reinforce the importance of using effective communication skills. Of course, at the start of the treatment one or both people might be very upset and need time and space to simply vent. However, even then the therapist can subtly start introducing the importance of using nonjudgmental language. Language needs to sound noncritical or nonblaming because the receiver may not come back if the sessions are too aversive. Obviously this will need to be titrated to the particular clients and situation. For example, if one person states, "You never pay any attention to me because you're always on that damn computer and I know that you are cheating on me," the receiver will perceive it as an attack and act defensively. As is common practice, the use of "I" statements allows for open communication of feelings in a nonjudgmental manner. An alternative would be to suggest that the prior statement be rephrased as, "I feel neglected when you spend long nights on the computer" or "I feel worried that you are involved sexually with others and I would feel more comfortable if you paid more attention to our relationship." This still allows for the one person to express their emotions and intensity but, at the same time, makes it more likely they will get a positive response back.

Practitioners should also help clients stay focused on one issue at a time and explain that long lists of complaints (so called "kitchen sinking") is often used to vent anger and disappointment but will likely lead the other to just shut down and withdraw. Similarly, it is helpful to avoid the use of negative trigger words and generalizations such as "always," "never," "should," or "must," which sound inflexible and invite heated rebuttal.

REDUCE SHAME. Shame is a major factor in any sexual acting out situation. Clients will need an opportunity to feel and to own their shame around what has occurred both as the perpetrator and as the victim. If sexual addiction and sexual codependency are present, the shame levels will be much higher and will have a longer history. The likelihood of sexual acting out as a trauma reenactment for both partners needs to be considered (Schwartz, Galperin, & Masters, 1995).

Use Empathetic Listening. Help clients listen fully and respectfully. Many spouses explain that they never sought cyberaffairs but found the process happening too fast for them to see and understand. Underneath, they may be feeling guilty and truly wish to stop. These clients would most likely fall into the "at-risk" category identified by Cooper, Putnam, et al. (1999). The cyberflings may have stirred up their own resentments about the pain over what's been missing for them in their marriage. If the offending partner tries to explain their motives for the affair, it is important to help the other partner suspend feelings of betrayal or loss of trust and listen to these explanations as openly as possible to maximize communication. If the couple discovers that the cyberaffair is the tip of the sexual addiction iceberg, there will be a cycle of shock, disbelief, and grief that needs to be worked through if they are to successfully stay together (Milrad, 1999; Carnes, 1991).

Consider Other Alternatives. If face-to-face communication and couples therapy is impossible and/or likely to further damage the relationship, then a period of individual therapy may be indicated. Young (1998b) suggests that other alternatives to help slow down the process and modulate the intensity might include adjuncts such as letter writing and even e-mail exchanges. Letter writing provides a longer period in which to allow thoughts and feelings to flow without interruption from a partner. Reading a letter in a less charged atmosphere may allow the other person to drop their defensive posture and respond in a more balanced manner. E-mail exchanges not only offer the same freedom from interruptions as letters but also can demonstrate to both people that the Internet can actually have a salubrious effect on a relationship. The couple may share a laugh at the irony of taking this approach, which could open the door to a more productive face-to-face talk (Young, 1998b).

If the couple is dealing with addictive issues, bibliotherapy (Griffin-Shelley, 1991) and support groups can be very important adjuncts to individual and/or couple treatment. The 12-step fellowships that developed the questionnaires listed above are available online as well as face to face. Cooper, Putnam, et al. (1999) and others encourage clinicians to have a fully developed, relapse prevention plan as a basic element in the treatment. Couples can work in their 12-step program on their own or in their therapy on this critical element in recovery. Again the Internet provides easy access to a special fellowship devoted to dealing with couples issues in recovery, Recovering Couples Anonymous or R.C.A. (http://www.recovering-couples).

Rebuild Marital Trust

As with any couple struggling in the aftermath of an affair, a major goal of the therapy is helping the couple to rebuild trust in the relationship. However, special care must be taken in relationship building after a cyberaffair because of three significant factors.

RULES FOR COMPUTER USE AT HOME. Unlike real-life affairs that may take place at the office, at a bar, or a hotel out of town, cyberaffairs often happen inside the couple's home. Young (1998a) suggests that the problem behavior centered on the computer so it now serves as a sign of infidelity and reminds the couple of past hurt. At the same time, a computer can also be a tool that is used for important nonrecreational purposes such as business activities or home finances. Simply removing the computer may not be a practical solution. Yet, each time the offending partner approaches the computer for a legitimate reason, it may trigger feelings of suspicion and jealousy for the other. In order to rebuild trust, it is important that the therapist help the couple evaluate how the computer will be used at home. Reasonable ground rules can be established such as moving the computer into a public area of the home. Blocking software and Internet Service Providers (ISPs), such as Integrity or Freedom that block adult sexual sites should be used. In cases of addiction, either a period of abstinence, or complete abstinence, from computer use may be necessary.

AVOID DEFENSIVENESS LIKE RATIONALIZING. Many times people will rationalize their behavior as just a fantasy or just typed words on a screen. They may contend that cybersex isn't "cheating" because of the lack of physical contact. Also, they may not have consciously gone on the Internet to look for a sexual and/or romantic experience, so they rationalize or minimize the impact of their behavior on the relationship. In order to help the couple move past the hurt and start to rebuild trust, therapists should be careful not to reinforce these rationalizations but focus on ways for them to take responsibility for their actions. In many instances, a great deal of defensiveness might be an indication that the behavior is part of a larger pattern of behavior that may include addiction. Addicts typically deny, rationalize, intellectualize, and project blame onto others (Griffin-Shelley, 1991), so some couples will need a great deal of support and therapy to deal with these seemingly overwhelming difficulties. Again, 12-step groups may be able to provide a level of support and structure beyond that which most therapists can offer.

RENEW COMMITMENT. The therapist should help the couple formulate relationship-enhancing goals that will renew commitment and improve intimacy. Forgiveness must be stressed. Care should also be taken to evaluate the types of activities the couple used to enjoy before the Internet and encourage them to engage in those events once again. As the couple identifies more with their "pre-Internet" life, positive feelings may emerge between the couple such as compassion, tenderness, and affection. At the same time, it must be clear that the final destination is not a return to the "old relationship" but instead a "new and improved" version. This is likely to entail taking select parts of the relation that were positive and initially attracted the people and mixing that with improved ways of dealing with past problems. In addition increasing both partners' awareness of potential problems and assisting them to develop skills and confidence to approach and resolve these before they can deteriorate into an affair. If abuse and addiction are part of the picture, couples can be supported and positively reinforced for reading, joining support groups, and learning the "tools of recovery" (Griffin-Shelley, 1991). Recovery may be difficult, but Schneider (1988), Manley (1999), and others have affirmed the possibility of change.

Underlying Issues

Cyberaffairs and cybersexual encounters can be a symptom of an underlying problem that existed in the relationship before the Internet ever entered the couple's lives. Common preexisting relationship problems include (a) poor communication skills, (b) unresolved sexual dissatisfaction, (c) differences in child-rearing practices, (d) a recent relocation from support from family and friends, (e) financial problems, and (f) poor conflict resolution skills. The presence of such issues will increase the risk of a cyberaffair because an online lover may offer the illusion of unconditional support and comfort to "help" the person who feels alienated in his or her relationship or marriage (Young, 1998a). A large segment (45%) of Cooper et al.'s (2000) sample fell into the "at-risk" group. In such cases, a person may use the cyberaffair as an easy escape or distraction from the hard task of dealing with ongoing issues. Internet sexual behaviors may also provide an outlet for unexpressed anger or dissatisfaction with the primary partner. Therefore, it is vital that therapists thoroughly assess and directly deal with possible underlying issues that may have contributed to the development of a cyberaffair.

In other cases, many couples report no significant marital problems prior to receiving a home computer and getting involved in a cyberaffair. Again, this parallels the Cooper et al. (2000) study that found 46% of their survey to be "recreational" or nonpathological users of online sexual material. These couples explain that after a few months, as they engage in a variety of Internet sexual experiences one partner may begin to make the comparison between an attractive online lover, who seems to fulfill every emotional need, and the current partner, who seems dull, routine, and boring in comparison. Ultimately, these cyber-relationships are typically revealed to be an unrealistic and self-created persona; however, they seem all too real inside the mind of the online user.

The risk of developing either an intermittent or recurrent problem stems from the subjective "fantasy" world that develops inside the mind of the person using the computer. The more the person fantasizes, the more he or she can exclude their significant real-life partner. The result can be a growing dissatisfaction with one's current real-life circumstances as the online fantasy intensifies in the user's mind. It is, therefore, important for a therapist to spend time with the couple understanding the ways in which the couple may have fallen short of each others' expectations and whether or not they are still investing energy into stretching themselves and the relationship to its fullest potential. When it turns out that one or both people imagine that they are in a "rut" and have hit a plateau, this needs to be challenged as does the unrealistic fantasy expectations that accompany most cyberaffairs.

Finally, as was found in the Cooper, Scherer et al. (1999) study, 8.5% of online users appear to manifest sexually compulsive features. Thus there is a significant minority of Internet users who are likely to be addicted to either the Internet, cybersex, cyber-relationships, or some combination of the three. In addition, their partners may also be at risk for codependency. These couples face many challenges. In addition to the compulsive behavior and the harm of the cyberaffair, they tend to have significant histories of abuse and addiction. For example, Carnes (1991) reported that the sex addicts that he studied came from backgrounds that included emotional abuse or neglect (98%), sexual abuse (80%), and/or physical abuse (75%). Several authors including Cooper, Putnam et al. (1999) have noted the prevalence of powerful comorbid disorders such as major depression, personality disorders, and posttraumatic stress disorder. Manley (1999) also indicated that chronic sexual dysfunction is a frequent occurrence in couples dealing with sexual addiction.

SUMMARY AND CONCLUSIONS

Cybersex and cyberaffairs present a new dimension in couple relationships. These computer-aided romantic and sexual behaviors were defined in the context of Internet use, abuse, and addiction (Cooper et al., 2000). Young's ACE model (1999) highlights the seductive power of anonymity, convenience, and opportunities for escape that possibly explains the existence of online infidelity. Implications for treatment were outlined from detection, to suggestions for improving communication and rebuilding trust. Because detection of online affairs can be difficult, a list of warning signs was presented and screening resources were listed. A number of practical steps were outlined to assist therapists in dealing with couples around the repercussions of a cyberaffair and to facilitate the rebuilding of trust within the relationship. Finally, underlying issues were examined for couples reporting normal marital difficulties, those having no prior problems, and those dealing with abuse and addictions. Clients and practitioners need to recognize that the Internet adds a new dimension in intimate relationships that has implications for assessment and treatment of couples who may, knowingly or unknowingly, be on the verge of a relationship meltdown due to the impact of cyberspace.

Future research is needed to more clearly delineate the identification and classification of problematic online sexual activities. Cooper, Putnam et al.'s (1999) proposed continuum of Internet sexual activities from life enhancing to pathological needs to be replicated and further refined. Problems like online sexual addiction, Internet and computer addiction, and online relationship dependency and/or virtual affairs are in need of further empirical study, as well as establishing and evaluating specific treatment strategies.

Obviously, much remains to be done in the "cyberfrontier" to more clearly understand its risks and benefits for online users, couples, and society as a whole.

REFERENCES

Brenner, V. (1997, August 18). *The results of an on-line survey for the first thirty days.* Paper presented at the 105th annual meeting of the American Psychological Association. Chicago, Illinois.

Carnes, P. (1991). *Don't call it love: Recovery from sexual addiction.* New York: Bantam.

Cooper, A. (1998a). Sexuality and the Internet: Surfing into the new millennium. *CyberPsychology & Behavior, 1*(2), 181–187.

Cooper, A. (1998b). Sexually compulsive behavior. *Contemporary Sexuality, 32*(4), 1–3.

Cooper, A., Delmonico, D., & Burg, R. (2000). Cybersex users, abusers, and compulsives: New findings and implications. *Sexual Addiction & Compulsivity, 7,* 5–29.

Cooper, A., Putnam, D. E., Planchon, L. A., & Boies, S. C. (1999). Online sexual compulsivity: Getting tangled in the net. *Sexual Addiction & Compulsivity, 6*(2), 79–104.

Cooper, A., Scherer, C., Boies, S. C., & Gordon, B. (1999). Sexuality on the internet: From sexual exploration to pathological expression. *Professional Psychology: Research and Practice, 30*(2), 154–164.

Cooper, A., & Sportolari, L. (1997). Romance in cyberspace: Understanding online attraction. *Journal of Sex Education and Therapy, 22*(1), 7–14.

Griffin-Shelley, E. (1991). *Sex and love: Addiction treatment and recovery.* New York: Praeger.

Griffiths, M. (1996). Technological addictions. *Clinical Psychology Forum, 76,* 14–19.

Griffiths, M. (1997, August 15). *Does Internet and computer addiction exist? Some case study evidence.* Paper presented at the 105th annual meeting of the American Psychological Association. Chicago, Illinois.

Manley, G. (1999). Treating chronic sexual dysfunction in couples recovering from sexual addiction and sexual coaddiction. *Sexual Addiction & Compulsivity, 6*(2), 111–124.

Milkman, H., & Sunderwirth, S. (1987). *Craving for ecstasy: The consciousness and chemistry of escape.* Lexington, MA: Lexington Books.

Milrad, R. (1999). Coaddictive recovery: Early recovery issues for spouses of sex addicts. *Sexual Addiction & Compulsivity, 6*(2), 125–136.

Morahan-Martin, J. (1997, August 18). *Incidence and correlates of pathological internet use.* Paper presented at the 105th annual meeting of the American Psychological Association. Chicago, Illinois.

Norwood, R. (1985). *Women who love too much.* Los Angeles, CA: Tarcher.

Quittner, J. (1997, April 14). Divorce Internet Style, *Time,* p. 72.

Scherer, K. (1997). College life online: Healthy and unhealthy Internet use. *Journal of College Development, 38,* 655–665.

Schneider, J. (1988). *Back from betrayal: Recovering from his affairs.* New York: Ballantine.

Schneider, J., & Schneider, B. (1999). *Sex, lies, and forgiveness.* Tucson, AZ: Resources Recovery Press.

Schwartz, M., Galperin, L., & Masters, W. (1995). Dissociation and the treatment of compulsive reenactment of trauma. In M. Hunter (Ed.), *Adult survivors of sexual abuse: Treatment and innovations* (pp. 42–55). Thousand Oaks, CA: Sage.

Shotton, M. (1991). The costs and benefits of "computer addiction." *Behavior and Information Technology, 10*(3), 219–230.

Young, K. S. (1997a, August 15). *What makes on-line usage stimulating? Potential explanations for pathological internet use.* Paper presented at the 105th annual meeting of the American Psychological Association. Chicago, Illinois.

Young, K. S. (1997b). The relationship between depression and Internet addiction. *Cyberpsychology and Behavior, 1*(1), 24–28.

Young, K. S. (1998a). Internet addiction: The emergence of a new clinical disorder. *CyberPsychology and Behavior, 1*(3), 237–244.

Young, K. S. (1998b). *Caught in the Net: How to recognize the signs of internet addiction and a winning strategy for recovery.* New York: John Wiley & Sons, Inc.

Young, K. S. (1999a) The evaluation and treatment of Internet addiction. In L. VandeCreek & T. Jackson (Eds.), *Innovations in clinical practice: A source book, Vol. 17* (pp. 19–31). Sarasota, FL: Professional Resource Press.

Young, K. S. (1999b). *Cybersexual addiction* [online]. Available. http://www.netaddiction.com/cybersexual_addiction.htm

Chapter 4

Children, Teens, and Sex on the Internet

ROBERT E. FREEMAN-LONGO

Sexual Abuse Prevention & Education Resources International, Bomoseen, Vermont, USA

With the growth of the number of Internet users and access to an increasing number of web sites and a variety of materials, there exists a concern about access to adult-oriented materials by underaged persons. This article uses Grounded Theory to address (a) the limited but growing knowledge of the area, (b) ways in which children and teens can access this material, (c) positives and negatives associated with developing online relationships that can become sexual, (d) the growing concerns regarding children's access to adult-oriented materials, and (e) the potential short- and long-term affects. This article also addresses recommendations for the future regarding ways to guide youth about the potential hazards associated with the use of online adult-oriented web sites, ways to reduce the incidence of children and teens accessing these materials, and useful prevention strategies.

INTRODUCTION

According to the American Medical Association, sexual abuse has reached epidemic proportions in the United States and is a serious public health problem (Freeman-Longo & Blanchard, 1998). Sexual abuse is a multifaceted problem that expands well beyond criminal sexual behavior. It is a continuum that on one end has relatively harmless acts such as the verbal sexual abuse by one of another (sexual harassing and/or sexualized comments), and on the other end the rape and murder of a human being.

When we think of sexual abuse we most often think about sexual crimes committed on persons, e.g., rape and child molestation. Sexual abuse, however, crosses many boundaries and does not always constitute (a) an illegal behavior or (b) a harmful act against another. Many people with sexual behavior problems are in fact abusive to others (rape, child sexual abuse), while others take advantage of people through their positions of trust or

Address correspondence to Robert E. Freeman-Longo, MRC, LPC, Sexual Abuse Prevention & Education Resources International, PO Box 467, Bomoseen, VT 05732-0467, USA. E-mail: robsaperi@aol.com authority (sexual harassment, a doctor having sexual relations with a patient, or a member of the clergy having sex with a trusting member of the church). Others engage in sexually abusive behaviors that may compromise themselves and others, e.g., women who engage in prostitution and the men who hire them for their services; sexual addicts who lose their jobs, homes, and families due to their addiction to pornography; adult entertainment; and the sex-for-sale industry (Freeman-Longo & Blanchard, 1998). In many cases, however, people with sexual behavior problems are individuals who frequently engage in sexual behavior that results in self-harm. These self-destructive, self-abusive behaviors may be both legal (the addiction to adult pornography or frequenting adult entertainment establishments) or illegal (the use, abuse, or addiction to child pornography and hiring prostitutes for sex).

In recent years, a new form of potentially self-destructive sexual behavior, and one which is legal for adults, has become more widely available to those who would use it. Access to the Internet, specifically access to pornographic and adult-oriented web sites, is on the rise in America (Cooper, Putnam, Planchon, & Boies, 1999).[1] Access to these web sites by children and teens also appears to be on the rise and is illegal. Sparse literature is available that addresses children and teens and their access to adult-oriented material online. Thus, there is no way to accurately assess the number of children and teens who go online daily, access adult-oriented materials, and enter adult-oriented chat rooms. Once online, an individual can pose as anyone of any age and any gender. There is no way to accurately determine if the person is being honest or deceptive unless there exists an offline relationship with that individual. An adult can go online, enter a chat room, and pretend to be a teenager and vice versa.

There are tens of thousands of web sites that are adult oriented and readily accessible to online users by simply typing the word "sex" in one of the many search engines available to Internet users. In fact, the word "sex" is one of the most frequently typed words in search engines. Depending upon one's online service provider, one may not necessarily have to search too far into "cyberspace" to look for these web sites and adult-oriented materials. America Online (AOL), the nation's largest Internet service provider, is a case in point. Without parental control, and depending on web sites accessed, the online subscriber can easily receive one or more e-mails per day inviting the subscriber to an adult-oriented web site. It simply requires the online subscriber to access one adult-oriented web site or enter an apparently harmless chat room provided to subscribers of AOL to initiate uninvited e-mail that takes the subscriber directly to adult-oriented sites. In fact, when the phrase "parental control" was typed in one search engine the result was not only a listing of parental control software ideas (the results showed 12,508 different

---

1. For the purposes of this article, "adult-oriented web sites" refers to web sites or services that include pornography, sexually oriented materials, adult dating services, and chat rooms that focus on explicit sexual conversation and cybersex activities.

sites), such as Net-Nanny, Cyber-Patrol, and Adequate.com, but also listed adult-oriented web sites such as Captain Cum's Weekly Pics and Nipples.net.[2]

Our modern day technology has many benefits, yet with those many benefits come many problems and potentially negative outcomes. Fortunate or unfortunate as the case may be, our media and technology have the ability to influence the public quickly and effectively. Those who pay attention to the media and use the available technology can both use it to their advantage and positive gain as well as abuse it to the point at which such use may result in personal loss and/or self-destructive behavior. Technology, access to the media, and accessing material available through the use of the Internet is a double-edged sword. Computers and, specifically, access to the Internet have the power to both draw people to it and create addictive behavior quickly and efficiently. Access to the Internet has the potential to both feed potential or existing addictions and skew one's sense of self and reality.

CHILDREN, TEENS, AND ADDICTION

Short of chemical dependency, which is a biologically based addiction that can occur at any age, and eating disorders, which often have their roots in psychologically based problems, we do not usually think of addictions afflicting children and teens. Rather, our images are often of drunken men and women, gamblers, drug addicts, and, over the past few decades, men and women who are sexual addicts. Little is known about sexual addiction and children and even less about children, teens, and sex on the Internet.

As a science we do not fully understand sexual addiction. There are some who challenge the idea that sexual addiction even exists (Carnes, 1989; Blanchard, 1997; Carnes, 1998). When it comes to children, teens, and sexual addiction, we are exploring uncharted territory. Given the relative newness of the sexual addiction field, we have many more questions than answers regarding the potential for young persons to develop sexual addiction. There are no long-term studies that tell us what can happen to a child who develops behavioral patterns and personal qualities associated with adult sexual addiction. We cannot predict what the potential short-term and long-term consequences may be if a young person develops these behavioral patterns and personality characteristics. At best, we can only speculate about what may occur based upon what we know about adults who develop sexual addiction and what the potential impacts are from online sexual addiction and experiences. What we do know is that children and teens can and do develop compulsive sexual behavior, e.g., masturbation (Ryan & Lane 1997; Barbaree, Marshall, & Hudson, 1993), and that sexual addiction may be pos-

---

2. http://www.webcrawler.com/cgi.bin/WebQuery?searchText=parental+controls (8/26/99)

sible given that compulsivity is often a precursor to addiction. Additionally, in writing this article I found there exists an increasing number of counselors and therapists seeing children and teens in their practice who come with problems associated with online sexual activities. Most have histories of previous problems that often serve as a catalyst for their online sexual activities.

In the absence of published literature and scientific knowledge about children, teens, and sex on the Internet, I have elected to pursue researching and thus writing this article using a Grounded Theory (GT) approach. GT does not begin with a hypothesis, but rather through social research a hypothesis evolves. GT is a research process that involves learning and taking direction as one moves forward in looking at a particular social issue. The active process of learning guides the researcher. Therefore, the following observations and case examples in this article are representative of what many of us believe is happening on the Internet when an individual, and specifically children and teens, becomes involved in online sexual activities. Because it is "illegal" for children and teens to go into adult-oriented web sites and problematic to engage in online sexual activities, many children and teens may be reluctant to openly and honestly disclose why they access adult-oriented web sites and services. They may be reluctant to tell us what they do, the details of their activities, to what degree they do it, what benefits they derive from it, and the frequency and time spent online engaging in sexual interests and activities. Therefore, at this point in time we may only have a snapshot of this particular area, while the big picture is more than likely very out of focus.

WHAT CHILDREN AND TEENS CAN ACCESS ONLINE

The Internet is a growing medium with thousands of new users signing on each year. According to 1997 statistics (Computerworld, 1998) estimates suggest that more than 15 million people use the Internet each day. Time online varies among users, and their initial purpose for going online (business vs. pleasure) also varies. As of 1997 there were more than 200 million web pages established for user perusal. Computerworld estimates that by 2001 there will be more than 94 million people accessing the Internet.

"Click here if you are 18 years of age or older." That is the familiar message one is greeted with when he or she is about to enter an adult-oriented web sites. However, there is no way to verify the actual age of the user and thus simply lying about one's age permits access to adult-oriented sites. Children and teens have access to a variety of adult-oriented web sites on the Internet. Chat rooms, pornography sites, adult video sites, and romance/dating services are but a few of the many and easily accessible adult-oriented materials to be found on the "information highway."

Pornographic web sites, those that involve both still photos and X-rated videos, are filled with every imaginable image and sexual act. The images are explicit and something can be found to meet anyone's particular sexual interests. Unfortunately, one can be assured that despite claims that all "models" are over the age of 18, many of the persons involved in the making of pornographic images are underage (Freeman-Longo & Blanchard, 1998). Therefore, it is easy for young people to recognize that many of these "models" are close to their age, thus legitimizing in the minds of the youth online that people their age are also involved in real-life and online sexual activities. It normalizes the experience. Children and teens often frequent such sites, as the following case illustrates.

> Chris is a 14-year-old male who has been convicted of sexually abusing his stepsister. He reports that he went online frequently to access pornographic materials. He visited the Playboy web site among others. On one occasion Chris viewed videos of women stripping as well as multiple still pictures of nude women.

In another case a young person in treatment wrote the following description of one of his online experiences after accessing the Internet on the computer at the local library. He was 13 at the time.

> It all started when I read an article in the newspaper about teens accessing pornography on the Internet. The next day after school, I went to the Library and went on the Internet and punched in *www.playboy.com*. After looking at this site I went to some pages of normal people that had nude women. About a month later there was a code on the computer so people could not access the pornography. I quickly figured it out and went to www.hustler.com. After looking through the pictures I talked with a person on the net [in a chat room offered by Hustler] about her body.[3]

Chat Rooms

Chat rooms have tremendous potential to attract and maintain one's interest in online sexual activities. They can be found almost anywhere one looks, including AOL, Excite, and other popular sites. Although some chat rooms indicate they are adult oriented, and one has to indicate he/she is 18 years of age or older to enter, many are not sex-oriented chat rooms. The chat topics seem harmless, but once inside anything can happen and sexual talk and innuendo is not uncommon regardless of the title of a particular chat room.

Many if not most of the chat rooms one easily finds online are filled with people claiming to be all ages and both sexes. Many chat room participants willingly share that they are underage (if in fact they are under age 18). They are young people looking for sex with anyone and will send a picture (even though there is no way to determine who is really in the picture). One can simply sit back and watch as people share sexual comments and explicit

---

3. If one visits the Hustler web site there is a Triple X chat room available for anyone to use.

statements or find someone who will engage you in cybersex activities privately.

AOL has hundreds of thousands of subscribers and is the largest Internet access carrier. As an AOL subscriber without parental controls, any child or teen can access numerous free chat rooms on assorted topics. Once in these rooms, children and teens are exposed to all types of sexual comments, sexual talk, and persons willing to trade pictures. If one visits these rooms there are many people claiming to be young (that is, in their early to mid-teens), however, none of the self-reported young persons responded to online inquiries as to why they are in the chat room (when asked why they are interested in sex), and many left the room immediately.

Many adult women report teen males trying to "hit" on them while in chat rooms. When asked about those experiences, several women replied that in fact they are hit on, in many instances multiple times while online, and that males claiming to be as young as 15 sent pictures (and offered to send nude pictures), asked for sex, sent uninvited e-mails, and tried to engage them in any type of sexual conversation. (Several women in one online chat room were skeptical when being asked about their experiences with teens, thinking the inquiries from me were actually coming from an underaged person and a guise to chat with them about sex!)

We must take the potential for children and teens to have access to undesirable materials in chat rooms seriously. As one professional notes,

> Based upon my experience in working with adolescents and sexual offenders, it is my opinion that the easiest way to obtain sexually related materials is via chat rooms. Pedophiles know this. Law enforcement has responded and frequently stings such pedophiles. It is also relevant to note that access to sexually related material may be accidental. Let me iterate that the chat room is clearly the best means for discussing/obtaining etc. sexually related material.[4]

POSITIVE ASPECTS OF ONLINE RELATIONSHIPS

There are many benefits that can be derived from the development of online relationships and online relationships that become sexual. The research (Cooper & Sportolari, 1997) suggests that the Internet can

1. facilitate the formation of romantic relationships,
2. improve the chances of finding an optimal partner,
3. develop relationships on attachments, not simply physical appearance, and
4. improve one's skills in interpersonal communication.

---

4. Amy Korzeniewski, personal communication, June 30, 1999.

With guidance and supervision, children and teens meeting people online their age can develop healthy and perhaps even advanced skills in interpersonal communication (see Cooper et al., 1999). Learning to express one's thoughts, feelings, and interests in the written word requires thought and the development of a skill that can be valuable in all life situations. However, left alone to meet anyone online, a child or teen can get into trouble as well as be exposed to undesirable language, propositions, and materials.

Problems with Online Relationships and Sex

There are potentially many more problems than benefits with the development of online relationships, and especially online relationships that are primarily for sexual purposes or become sexual. These problems may be magnified for youth who do not have the knowledge, experience and maturity to self-assess what is okay and what is getting out of hand in regard to their personal lives. Some of these problems include but are not limited to the following:

1. Many online relationships are not based in reality; what they read and see about people, relationships, and sex is distorted.
2. Many users begin to seek higher levels of excitement, as current experiences result in a lack of gratification (their tolerance levels change and/or they become satiated to particular activities).
3. With some youth there may be the potential to increase sexual drive and urges resulting in possible compulsive and/or addictive behavior. When this occurs healthy sexual drive may no longer be exciting. This is especially problematic for youth who engage in sexually abusive and aggressive behaviors.
4. For underaged persons such activities may increase the youths' sexual desire for in-person sex and thus result in earlier real-life sexual experiences.

We know that many youth now entering therapy with problems of online sexual activity and other problematic sexual behaviors are already in trouble in some aspect of their lives. The potential to exacerbate the above noted problems and develop more serious problems including sexual compulsivity and possible sexual addiction may soon follow if left untreated.

Warning Signs that a Child or Teen May Be Moving into Sexual Addiction on the Internet

According to Cooper et al. (1999) the following are indicators of addiction to and may serve, in the absence of scientifically validated studies on youth, as potential indicators for online sexual addiction of youth. Some of these warning signs include the following:

1. excessive use of the Internet, including neglect of personal relationships and isolation,
2. acute/chronic depression,
3. seeking repeated mood-altering experiences that have brought about "highs,"
4. sense of pseudointimacy,
5. Internet serves as an outlet for unresolved sexual difficulties and unfocused sexual energy,
6. children and adolescents with histories of sexual behavior problems may be more prone to engage in these activities,
7. children and teens who do not engage in any or few peer-related social activities.

According to Young and Rogers (1998), there appears to be a correlation between time online and negative consequences. When a child or teen is spending more than one or two hours at a time online, we should be concerned (see Cooper et al., 1999).

Software and Parental Controls to Block Access on the Internet to Sexual Materials, Violence, and Other Undesirable Topics

The rise in numbers of children going online has resulted in software companies and others devising a variety of programs and tools that limit a child's access to materials that parents or those in positions of authority have determined are inappropriate for children. Unfortunately, many children are now more skilled than their caretakers and overseers in the use of computers and technology.[5] Many young people are skilled enough in computer science and technology to be able to access secure and sensitive information online and can break the codes that protect federal information and sensitive materials (hackers). With such knowledge, skills, and abilities, these young people can more easily work around software and other devices that attempt to limit their access to material on the Internet. Once done, they can easily share their secrets with peers.

For those professionals who work with children and adolescents, growing numbers of cases appear to be revealing themselves. One professional notes,

> My experience with teens and sex on the Internet has taught me the following:
> 1. Chat rooms provide opportunity for teens to send each other pictures (of all sorts).

---

5. In my child's school (elementary) I was asked this school year to sign a release for him to use the Internet with the understanding of the potential risks for him to come across materials that would be objectionable for children of his age group.

2. Pornographic businesses will often send "free," but limited, access to materials through those chat rooms.

3. The teen does not have to request these materials to receive them.

4. Internet providers are not timely in responding to complaints from parents.

5. You may have to remove the teen from Internet access for a while (consequences of behavior, changing circle of friends on Internet, etc.).

6. Links to pornography and sex can be found everywhere; you can't block access. I found explicit pictures depicting sexual acts on my favorite recipe web site![6]

Another professional stated,

I have worked with a couple of kids who got into the Internet sex sites by using their parent's credit cards and birth dates. Easily done . . . wallet left on dresser, pull out credit card, write down number [and expiration date], put credit card and wallet back.[7]

In my research on this issue I have found that many of the software packages to block access to sexual, violent, or other materials and parental controls may not work and/or can be easily gotten around by youth. The following professional who works with children and teens and has children of his own illustrates this point:

I have a 14-year-old son who is very good with computers. I put Cyber-Patrol on his machine, and like this so far. It tracks where he goes. I had Net-Nanny, but it blocks with a dialog box across 3/4 of the screen, but [one] can beat it. I can't beat Cyber-Patrol and so far, he can't either. He wants to chat but we block that (and the newsgroups) with filtered access to the web.[8]

Another writes,

Net-Nanny and similar programs can block access to the newsgroups identified as being pornographic. The problem is that anyone can post a pornographic image or story to nonpornographic newsgroups [as cited in the cases below]. Filtering software can also be bypassed, as new sites are being created daily. Similarly, newsgroups can be accessed on the web, at sites such as http://www.dejanews.com and http://www.remarq.com.[9]

One professional shared a story about a creative teen who did the following:

I had a case where a 16-year-old, who had a history of phone sex (thousands of dollars) placed a camcorder, hidden, to record the combination

---

6. Mary Helen Walker, personal communication, June 30, 1999.
7. Gerry Blasingame, personal communication, June 30, 1999.
8. James LaBundy, personal communication, June 30, 1999.
9. Brian Major, personal communication, July 7, 1999.

of the safe, where his father kept the code to the computer. He got the code and got into porn sites. Talk about ingenuity.[10]

Sometimes the results of such actions by teens have horrific endings as another professional describes:

> A teen in our community was selling child porn he downloaded off the Internet. I don't know too much about the case as his attorney blocked him having to come into the treatment program. The kid committed suicide three weeks later, after intense harassment from his peers at high school as the word got around very quickly.[11]

Children have access to computers in a variety of places both in and out of the home. Not all computers are programmed with childproof software, blocks, and controls including those in public schools, libraries, parent's workplaces, and those in the homes of friends and relatives. The following case examples illustrate the potential for easy access.

> In one public school a student was instructed by the teacher to pull up the local newspaper. This newspaper had the word "Star" in its name, a common word in the title of many newspapers much like Chronicle and Journal. The student typed in the newspaper's name ("The ____ ____ Star") and a graphic photograph of a couple having sexual relations came up on the screen.

> Another case example involves a child working with an adult researching golden retrievers online. The child typed in "golden retriever" and was met with a screen that addressed "golden showers," a practice which involves couples having sexual relations and one or both persons urinating on their sexual partner.

As noted from cases and text above there are several software programs available to parents, educators, and others, but one must not put complete faith in them as foolproof methods of limiting access to unwanted materials on the Internet. The best guide for parents, caretakers, and others is to test these programs first. One professional notes his experience:

> When a site is hit (detected) by some parental control software, about 60–75% of the browser screen area is covered with a warning area black. I could see "around" it, and was able to get rid of it by trying random toggles (i.e., shift-tab, etc.). I don't remember which one deleted it, as I stopped and looked for another program immediately.[12]

---

10. John Pacult, private practice. Personal communication, July 2, 1999.
11. Gerry Blasingame, private practice. Personal communication, July 2, 1999.
12. James LaBundy, personal communication, July 1, 1999.

Prevention

There are several things we can do to minimize childrens' access to the Internet and specifically their accessing undesirable materials and adult-oriented web sites. Some of the suggestions mentioned above will be reviewed again. First and foremost, however, it is necessary to understand that any successful prevention program regardless of the issue requires education. Professionals, educators, and others must work hard to educate parents, caregivers, libraries, schools, youth organizations, and those who would provide children with access to the Internet about the potential hazards and the best ways to avoid them.

Children and teens are naturally curious about sex and will seek out sexual information and stimuli. Parents, educators, and caregivers need not panic when they discover a child's or teen's natural curiosity and exploration. Instead they can use such times when children and teens ask questions or are found engaging in curious exploration such as looking at adult erotica or surfing the Internet as "teachable moments." They can be guided to age-appropriate materials, books, or sites on the Internet. For example, in the above example where the child finds "golden showers" instead of "golden retrievers," an appropriate response might be, "There is nothing wrong with the human body and nudity. However, when pictures or writing portray abuse, aggression, humiliation, or otherwise degrade the human body, then it is not healthy to spend time looking at these materials."

If a child finds adult materials at home or accidentally sees a parent looking at adult-oriented materials such as *Playboy*, a response such as the one below can be helpful. Remember, honesty in this area is the best policy.

> I know you have seen my *Playboy* magazines/saw me looking at my *Playboy* magazines (and/or I too have seen the *Playboy* web site). As your father I still prefer you wait a few more years to look at these materials/to go to these sites, but I want you to know what I think about these sites and why I feel this way. There is important information teenagers and adults need to have about human sexuality and sexual behavior. These sources of information do not always provide accurate information nor the best education regarding sex and sexual behavior.

We must educate children and teens with age-appropriate materials that are factual and honest. We cannot assume that all children understand the illegality of child pornography, downloading illegal materials, the potential harm of using pornography and other adult-oriented materials, and the potential problems associated with meeting people online and the dangers of meeting them in person. Younger children and even teens may need supervision when going online. One professional makes the following comments and suggestions:

> It is easy for teens to access [sexual materials on the web], and it may not even have been planned. A simple spelling error or an innocent search for information can lead to entry into areas that are less than desirable.

In reviewing our lab on a regular basis, it is amazing the number of times sites appear, and when you look at the reference you can tell that the student was looking for information other than what appeared. Some of these sites are difficult to break out of without shutting the machine completely down.

Innocent wanderings into such topics as "zip" (looking for zip codes), "tattoos," "Whitehouse," and "doanload" (instead of "download") have taken students places they did not want to be and the list goes on.

Even with careful monitoring it is very easy for anyone using the Internet to access areas where they really do not want to be and do so believing they are going into something they wanted to look up.[13]

There are several steps parents, educators, and others can take to maximize a child's or teen's fun and learning on the Internet while avoiding most of the associated risks of online activity.

First, don't put computers with Internet access in a child's room. Instead keep the computer with Internet access in a public place with lots of activity at home and where the use can be easily monitored, such as a family room or kitchen. Children and teens are less likely to do the forbidden when they know you are present. In addition it is an excellent time to talk about what the child is learning or is curious about and to guide him/her to age-appropriate sites.

Next, test software that claims to block children's access to adult-oriented materials on the Internet. Be a good consumer: check what are the comparative ratings, which are the most popular. See if you can beat it . . . if you can, your child may be able to as well. Look for updates, new versions, or new software frequently. Ask other parents what they use.

Finally, provide children and teens with age-appropriate alternatives. AOL, for example, has a teen romance chat room that is monitored for content. Help your child explore what is out there in cyberspace. Visit a variety of sites with your child online. You are bound to come across undesirable sites, and that can become a valuable "teaching moment" as you discuss what is good and bad about the site.

Of course, one question that needs to be answered at this time asks if young persons know that accessing and downloading some of the materials from the Internet (other than posted warnings on some sites that are adult oriented) is illegal. If these children and teens do not fully understand the illegality, risks, and consequences of accessing and/or downloading these materials, how do they gain responsible and accurate information about what is illegal and what is legal? This may very well be why this problem may be growing and is possibly greater than we know. Such education and information dissemination is, of course, the basis for primary prevention.

Prevention, simply defined, is the effort to prevent a particular problem before it occurs. Health may be defined as the condition of being sound in body, mind, and spirit, and free of disease or psychological problems. Public

---

13. Anonymous, personal communication, June 30, 1999.

health is a community/societal effort to promote the safety and well-being of one's health. Successful prevention requires the honest education of the public regarding a particular problem including defining the problem, determining its prevalence in society, identifying the risk factors for that problem, identifying ways to reduce and prevent risk factors, and evaluating the effectiveness of the prevention efforts and interventions used. The media is currently used to promote worthwhile causes and prevention messages for many societal problems. We can use the media to help with public education and prevention efforts, and to counter the negative media messages and images that contribute to the problem of unhealthy sexual practices, including sexual addiction.

In order to reduce and then prevent the incidence of children and teens accessing adult-oriented sexual materials online, there are several steps we can take. First we must recognize that as parents, teachers, educators, and other professionals we have an obligation to work on prevention efforts and use methods that have a history of proven efficacy. Scare tactics, misinformation based upon myth, personal bias, and narrowly focused issues, especially those that are not scientifically proven to be effective or those that have proven via scientific method to be ineffective, must not be used. These methods will not deter or stop youth who are wise to the ways of such models and methods. Nor are negative messages and punishment likely to be effective as such methods have historically demonstrated they are not effective in prevention efforts.

What do we do then? We use methods and campaigns that demonstrate the ability to be seen, heard, and believed by others and then hopefully incorporate them into the lives of people who are seeking help. No one method is foolproof, but the more methods we try over time the more likely the information is to be used. Some of the proven methods include but are not limited to the following.

1. Outreach: Many people are faced with these issues. Forming a local committee through the schools or youth service organizations can help spread the word and assist parents, educators, and others in learning about this issue and how to prevent children and teens from getting into trouble on the Internet. Booths at school functions and other child-focused activities are examples of ways to get visibility. Pamphlets on the issue are easy to design and have printed.
2. Public service announcements: Sometimes local television stations, radio stations, and newspapers are willing to air/print public service announcements from local groups, organizations, and committees.
3. Use of Internet advertising and web sites to educate young people about the potential hazards and possible addiction to adult-oriented sexual material: If enough parents, educators, and people write to the Internet service providers such as AOL, Microsoft, and local access providers, it just may influence these businesses to put public service announcements and alternative child information online as ads.

4. Warnings put on adult-oriented web sites about the potential to develop sexual compulsivity and addiction by users: This is a more difficult task, as these businesses are out to make money any way they can. We can encourage them to post warnings on these sites much like we do on cigarettes and alcohol (Freeman-Longo & Blanchard, 1998).

5. Healthy sexual messages: We need to encourage schools, youth service organizations and other media that caters to children and teens to put out messages that are focused on healthy sexuality. There are many current issues facing our children today. Sexual harassment, sexual abuse, and sex on the Internet are just a few topics that can be the focus of public service announcements and other media messages that discourage unhealthy sexual behavior.

6. The use of case examples in public service announcements and healthy sexual messages: Much like we have seen and still see in ads targeting drug abuse, drunk driving, and AIDS, we can encourage the use of real-life case examples that depict children and teens that have suffered serious consequences and personal problems as a result of online activities, etc.

7. Public education that includes messages that are honest, factual, address the pros and cons of accessing such material, and information that addresses the potential consequences for repeated and/or addictive use of the Internet: Youth programs that have been most successful use accurate, honest information. We cannot underestimate the knowledge of young people. Misinformation turns them off.

In addition we can and encourage others to do the following.

1. Teach children, teens, and others about the incidence of credit card fraud on the Internet—Children need to understand that putting credit card numbers online can result in thousands of dollars in charges by people who "steal" the credit card numbers because not all web sites are secure.

2. Teach children and teens to never give out personal information on the Internet: Give examples of people who have done that and been kidnapped or harassed endlessly as a result of disclosing such information.

3. Advise youth to never meet people in person whom they have met online: Again, advise them of the cases that have resulted in people being kidnapped, assaulted, and even murdered.

4. Advise youth that there is no complete privacy on the Internet: Many people either don't know or don't understand that the Internet does not provide absolute privacy and/or safety. Anything that they write or do can be traced and can lead to problems.

5. Put computers with Internet access in public places such as kitchens, dining rooms, etc., and not in children's rooms: As noted above, children and teens are less likely to engage in forbidden activities when they are being closely monitored and parents take an active interest and/or role in what the child is doing.

6. Use software that provides the best security and precaution against accessing adult-oriented web sites, including those that will track the child's use of the Internet and sites visited. Look for updated versions and newer/improved software periodically. AOL is an Internet user service that provides both parental controls and the ability to track where the user has been online.

7. When a child violates the rules and conditions set by parents and caregivers for using the Internet, remove the child's privilege of Internet access, including if necessary prohibiting him/her from going to friend's homes, libraries, schools, etc., with Internet access.

SUMMARY

We currently lack scientific research and information regarding children, teens, and sexual activity on the Internet. Further, we are uncertain about their potential to become sexual compulsives or even sexual addicts if they engage in these online behaviors. The American Psychological Association has determined exposure to TV violence is impacting children and their aggressive behaviors in negative ways. We should be equally as cautious about children's exposure to sexual materials on the Internet.

Because the short- and long-term impact of children engaging in these activities is not known, we must be cautious about how we proceed in gathering this information and think about the presumed current risks associated with this behavior. The risks as we understand them now include

1. exposure to incorrect information about human sexual behavior,
2. exposure to age-inappropriate sexual materials,
3. the potential to develop sexually compulsive behavior, and
4. the potential to develop sexual addiction.

These potential personal harms appear to outweigh any potential benefits from engaging in online sexual activities. This article serves as a call to recognize this behavior as a problem, encourage dedicated research into further understanding it, and to encourage prevention efforts to help children, teens, parents, teachers, and others understand the potential risks and harm to children engaging in these behaviors while discouraging use of the Internet for sexual purposes.

Finally, there are issues that warrant further research in this area. First, in a population of children exposed to online pornography and adult-oriented materials, can we differentiate factors of emotional vulnerability and other personality traits that would predispose some to become sexual compulsives and potentially sexual addicts? Second, does online sexual behavior/activity predispose some children and teens to act out sexually and/or engage in sexually abusive behaviors? Third, are there effective ways professionals and others can prevent children and teens from accessing such materials or minimizing the extent to which they do? Certainly there are many more issues to be addressed as we learn more about this potentially serious and damaging problem facing youth.

REFERENCES

Barbaree, H. E., Marshall, W. L., & Hudson, S. M. (Eds.) (1993). *The juvenile sex offender.* New York: The Guilford Press.

Blanchard, G. T. (1997). Introduction. *Sexual Addiction & Compulsivity, 4*(1),1–2.

Computerworld. (1998). *Commerce by numbers - Internet population* [Online]. Available: http://www.computerworld.com/home/Emmerce.nsf/All/pop

Carnes, P. (1989). *Contrary to love: Helping the sexual addict.* Minneapolis, MN CompCare Publishers.

Carnes, P. (1998). Editorial: The presidential diagnosis. *Sexual Addiction & Compulsivity, 5*(3),153–158.

Cooper, A., Putnam, D. E., Planchon, L. A., & Boies, S. C. (1999). Online sexual compulsivity. *Sexual Addiction, 6*(2), 79–104.

Cooper, A., & Sportolari, L. (1997). Romance in cyberspace: Understanding online attraction. *Journal of Sex Education and Therapy, 22*(1), 7–14.

Freeman-Longo, R. E., & Blanchard, G. T. (1998). *Sexual abuse in America: Epidemic of the 21st century.* Brandon, VT: Safer Society Press.

Ryan, G., & Lane, S. (Eds.) (1997). *Juvenile sexual offending: Causes, consequences, and correction.* San Francisco: Jossey-Bass Publishers.

Young, K. S., & Rogers, R. C. (1998). The relationship between depression and Internet addiction. *CyberPsychology & Behavior, 1*(1), 25–28.

Chapter 5

Online Sexual Addiction and Compulsivity: Integrating Web Resources and Behavioral Telehealth in Treatment

DANA E. PUTNAM

Online Sexual Addiction: Education, Support, and Resources,
San Luis Obispo, California, USA

MARLENE M. MAHEU

California School of Professional Psychology, San Diego, California, USA

Technology is changing the nature of problems people are having as well as how we treat them. This article discusses how factors associated with use of the Internet may initiate and maintain sexually compulsive behavior online. Ways to make use of web resources in the treatment of online sexual addiction and compulsivity are suggested. Behavioral Telehealth, a possible avenue for conducting psychotherapy using communications technology, is introduced. Ethical, legal, and regulatory issues relevant to using communications technology to practice psychotherapy are reviewed.

It is well recognized that some people have problems managing their sexual behavior on the World Wide Web (Cooper, Putnam, Planchon, & Boies, 1999; Cooper, Scherer, Boies, & Gordon, 1999; Delmonico, 1997; Greenfield, in press; Leiblum, 1997; Putnam, 1999). Recent research indicates that those termed "cybersex addicts" spend an estimated 15 to 25 hours per week online pursuing sexual material (Cooper, Delmonico, & Burg, 2000). Some of these individuals have had sexual behavior problems in the past in a variety of other settings, while others have only recently developed problems in relation to their use of online sexual material. Due to the specific nature of the Internet, there appear to be individuals who develop compulsive sexual behavior who would not have otherwise developed a problematic sexual behavior. These individuals have been termed "at-risk" users of the Internet (Cooper, Putnam et al., 1999). At-risk users spend up to an estimated 10 hours per week online pursuing sexual material (Cooper et al., 2000).

At-risk users are vulnerable to factors that make online sexual content

Address correspondence to Dana E. Putnam, P.O. Box 13602, San Luis Obispo, CA 93406, USA. E-mail: drputnam@onlinesexaddict.org especially tempting. Factors that have contributed to the lure of sexual content on the Internet include what has been referred to by Cooper and colleagues (1998; Cooper, Putnam et al., 1999; Cooper, Scherer et al., 1999) as the "Triple-A Engine" (i.e., accessibility, affordability, and anonymity) as well as behavioral factors such as classical and operant conditioning (Putnam, 1997b, 1999). An understanding of the role played by these factors is important when developing treatment approaches to deal with online sexual addiction and compulsivity, and when using treatment resources available on the web.

FACTORS THAT CONTRIBUTE TO THE ESTABLISHMENT AND MAINTENANCE OF COMPULSIVE ONLINE SEXUAL BEHAVIOR

In examining the establishment of compulsive online sexual behavior we will first review primary factors that are thought to be etiologically associated with sexual addiction and compulsivity. These factors may be thought of as vulnerabilities that relate to why particular individuals are especially susceptible to developing problems with compulsive sexuality. Once traditionally considered etiological considerations are reviewed, we will then examine the role the Triple-A Engine and behavioral factors play in making the Internet environment risky for vulnerable individuals.

Primary Etiological Considerations

A multitude of factors have been discussed as being etiologically associated with the development of compulsive sexual behavior. Sexual addiction and compulsivity may develop as part of a response to past physical, sexual, family, and social trauma (Carnes, 1993; Robinson, 1999; Schwartz, 1992; Tedesco & Bola, 1997; Whitfeld, 1998) and family sexual behavior and attitudes (Anderson & Coleman, 1991; Earle & Earle, 1995). Hypersexuality has been hypothesized to be etiologically related to biological factors such as testosterone and serotonin levels (Bradford, 1997; Grubin & Mason, 1997; Kafka & Prentky, 1992). Further, personality disorders (Rickards & Laaser, 1999), mood and anxiety disorders (Coleman, 1992; Earle & Earle, 1995; Kafka & Prentky, 1992), and substance abuse and dependence (Carnes, 1991; Sealy, 1999) have all been discussed as comorbid conditions associated with sexual addiction and compulsivity. These factors have been particularly relevant to those individuals who have shown an established pattern of out-of-control sexual behavior over time. It is unclear at this time, however, to what degree these factors also apply to at-risk individuals who were not sexually compulsive prior to using the Internet

It appears that at-risk individuals have many of the same underlying vulnerabilities as sexual compulsives, though possibly less severe. As noted by Cooper, Putnam et al. (1999), at-risk individuals may be vulnerable to developing a problem due to depressive symptoms and difficulty coping with stress. At-risk individuals with no prior sexually compulsive behavior appear to have been able to cope with their problems without becoming sexually compulsive prior to discovering online sexual material, but factors unique to the Internet resulted in them engaging in sexual behavior that interfered in their life.

The Triple-A Engine

As noted by Cooper et al. (1998; Cooper, Putnam et al., 1999; Cooper, Scherer et al., 1999), accessibility, affordability, and anonymity can facilitate the use of the web for sexual purposes. Pornography and opportunities to interact with others via text, audio, and video are easily accessible to almost anyone with an Internet connection. Further, a significant amount of online sexual material is available at no charge or nominal fees (Hapgood, 1996; Cooper, Putnam et al., 1999).

Accessibility and affordability provide the opportunity to explore sexuality online. Yet probably the most significant factor that engages at-risk users is anonymity. The online user is not physically seen and may consider himself to be undetectable to others. While one's identity online is not always anonymous, many people make the erroneous assumption that when online they operate within a cloak of anonymity. Therefore, individuals who would not otherwise allow themselves to be seen in adult bookstores, strip clubs, or buying sexual material at the local liquor store feel safe exploring sexual material and activities online.

Behavioral Factors

While the Triple-A Engine may facilitate involvement with online sexual material, behavioral factors can maintain that behavior. Once a person has begun to engage in online sexual activity, behavioral factors can combine with individual vulnerabilities to establish and maintain problematic online sexuality. Individual vulnerabilities such as anxiety, depression, stress, and interpersonal difficulties may increase a person's susceptibility to behavioral conditioning because the online sexual behavior temporarily removes the dysphoric state (Cooper, Putnam et al., 1999; Putnam, 1997b, 1999). Thus, the sexual behavior is reinforced both because of the physiological response and because of the temporary psychological relief the response provides.

The process of becoming conditioned to have sexual arousal in relation to computer use is akin to the conditioning process discussed by Junginger (1997) in relation to fetishism. Junginger explained how the fetish object becomes associated with sexual arousal and masturbation. Sexual arousal and masturbation result in positive reinforcement due to the physical sexual stimulation and release that occurs with orgasm. Negative reinforcement also occurs if the sexual arousal and masturbation relieves a negative emotional state, such as anxiety.

As with fetish objects, repeated pairings of computer use and sexual arousal can result in classically conditioned sexual arousal to the computer (Putnam, 1997b, 1999). As a result, simply sitting down to work at the computer can start a sexual response that may facilitate online sexual activities. The powerful effect of operant conditioning may increase and maintain the behavior. With operant conditioning a behavior (e.g., computer use for sexual purposes) is reinforced by the results of that behavior (e.g., sexual arousal and orgasm). Operant conditioning occurs in individuals who have problems with online sexuality because their online sexual activities usually result in masturbation and orgasm and relieve a dysphoric state. Therefore, treatment can be improved by taking measures to (a) counter the conditioning effects, and (b) ameliorate the underlying vulnerabilities.

USING THE WORLD WIDE WEB TO FACILITATE TREATMENT

Traditionally, psychological treatment has been provided by mental health providers in an office environment while communicating face to face with the patient. Technology is starting to change this tradition. With the advent of the Internet, people have begun to seek help on the web, and some mental health providers have begun to offer web-based interventions (Cutter, 1996; Maheu & Gordon, 1999). People are now looking for help for their psychological distress on mental health-oriented web sites, bulletin boards, e-mail groups, and chat rooms. Many of these people are looking for help because they, or their spouse or partner, have a problem related to compulsive sexual behavior on the Internet For example, from July 1998 to July 1999 a web site that provides education, support, and resources to people concerned about their own or another's online sexual behavior had over 1.5 million files accessed and over 7,000 messages posted to the site's bulletin boards (see http://onlinesexaddict.org/wusage and http://onlinesexaddict.org/bb.html).

Online resources have the advantage of being more accessible than traditional adjuncts to therapy. Most web resources are available any time of day, thus allowing for the use of resources when distress is experienced and motivation for change is greatest. In addition, individuals with stigmatizing or embarrassing problems are more easily able to acknowledge their problems and receive support on the Internet due to the degree of anonymity offered by online resources (Putnam, 1998).

It is important to note that we view the use of e-mail, chat rooms, bulletin boards and newsgroups as beneficial adjuncts to therapy, but they are not sufficient for treatment of sexually compulsive individuals. Psychotherapy was developed on the premise that the practitioner can see and hear the patient. Psychotherapists are taught to use visual and auditory cues in order to accurately diagnose and appropriately treat their patients. Psychotherapy in a virtual environment that is void of visual and auditory cues (e.g., e-mail and chat rooms) is at best risky and at worst harmful. When Internet capabilities expand to deliver high quality video and audio interaction, practitioners will be able to use these technologies to provide psychotherapy.

Description of Online Recovery Resources

Recovery resources on the web include newsgroups, e-mail groups, chat rooms, and web sites that provide information, services, and products related to sexual addiction recovery (Cooper, Putnam et al., 1999; Delmonico, 1997). Resources that provide the opportunity to interact with others online involve either synchronous or asynchronous communication. Synchronous communication occurs in "real time." That is, with synchronous communication people can connect to the Internet and interact with each other immediately, exchanging information within seconds. With asynchronous communication, messages are sent to people or posted online and can be retrieved at the recipient's convenience.

Newsgroups are a type of asynchronous communication where people can post text messages in an online forum that others can respond to. These forums have the advantage of being accessible and free, and they exist on almost every imaginable topic, including sexual addiction. A serious problem with sexual addiction newsgroups is that they are heavily targeted by Internet pornography businesses. In the newsgroups devoted to sexual addiction it is typical to see more pornography postings than postings of appropriate material dealing with recovery. An alternative to newsgroups is bulletin boards on web sites that are monitored and kept free from inappropriate postings. Bulletin boards on web sites are similar in structure to newsgroups and also are a form of asynchronous communication.

E-mail groups are associations of individuals who communicate in an asynchronous manner via e-mail. These groups are usually run by a system referred to as a "listserv." When e-mail is sent to the addresses on the listserv every person in the group receives the e-mail communication. Listserv groups may be used to discuss sexual addiction issues and provide a form of social support for group members. Listserv e-mail groups may be used to facilitate the development of a cyber community that supports its members during times of crisis. Participation in such groups may be used as part of a relapse prevention plan to cope with urges to act out sexually. Twelve-step programs can also make use of e-mail. Individuals can work through the 12-steps as part of an e-mail group and use e-mail to correspond with their sponsor and group members.

Newsgroups, bulletin boards, and e-mail have the benefit of being available 24 hours a day. Whenever there is the need, individuals can use these forums to write out thoughts and feelings, knowing that others will see what they write and may respond to them. These resources, however, do not allow for synchronous communication, which is the benefit of using chat rooms. Chat rooms are used for live text-based conversations. In a chat room two or more individuals can meet, write, and respond to each other in real time. Chat is being used for online groups (e.g., 12-step meetings) and for educational purposes.

It is important for users of online resources to be aware that much of the information obtained in face-to-face contact is absent from text-based communication. For example, vocal and nonverbal visual cues are eliminated. Thus, inherent to chat and e-mail is a high risk for miscommunication, and individuals are more likely to project their own biases into interactions when written information is ambiguous. It appears that at the present time the use of text-based resources is most appropriate for provision of information, support, and as part of a relapse prevention plan but not for the direct provision of psychological services by mental health professionals.

Synchronous communication using audio and video is increasing online. People are connecting cameras to their computers and projecting live images of themselves over the Internet Audio and video is already being used by pornography businesses online, but the potential exists to use these forms of communication therapeutically as well. The use of videoconferencing technology for psychotherapy is discussed further in the section on Behavioral Telehealth.

Initiating and Maintaining Abstinence

The web is an important resource to consider when treating people who have problems managing their sexual behavior. Recovery-oriented web sites, bulletin boards, and chat rooms can be used to provide education, support, and diversion from sexual acting out. The use of online resources may be incorporated into relapse prevention plans to provide individuals with behavioral alternatives to compulsive sexuality. Additional technology-based strategies include the use of Internet service providers (ISPs) and filtering software to prevent access to pornographic web sites (Cooper, Putnam et al., 1999; Delmonico, 1997; Putnam, 1997b, 1999).

It is important to state however that there are inherent problems with using online resources in the treatment of problematic online sexuality. Directing a sexually compulsive person to seek help online when this is where the problem occurs could be thought of as akin to holding an Alcoholics Anonymous meeting in a bar. Thus, it could be argued that sexually compulsive Internet users need to simply stop using the computer. While such an approach may be temporarily necessary, we agree with Young (1999) that for many such an approach is not practical. This is because the Internet has become a commonly used technology in business and will likely someday be as prevalent as the telephone. Therefore, it seems appropriate to include treatment that addresses the problem where it occurs, online.

Ideally, treatment will include and be based on actual face-to-face contact with a qualified mental health professional who can complete a full assessment and assist in the development of a relapse prevention plan that makes use of available technology and online resources. The development of such a plan should take into account the factors discussed earlier (i.e., access, affordability, anonymity, and behavioral conditioning) and how technology and resources can reduce the power of these factors. One way to approach developing such a plan could be conceptualized as developing lines of defense.

The first line of defense is used to deal with the issues of access, affordability, anonymity, and breaking the behaviorally conditioned cycle. The second line of defense refers to strategies to use to maintain abstinence. These strategies can be used when a person is at risk for lapse or relapse and alternative means of coping are needed.

As part of the first line of defense the clinician can counter the apparent affordability and anonymity of online sexual behavior. Information can be elicited about how interaction with sexual content online has cost the person money and time, reduced their productivity at work, and/or damaged their relationships. Also, it may be helpful to shatter the myth of online anonymity by pointing out that computer savvy people can discover the identity of people online. In fact, there are organizations on the Internet that perform investigations to obtain information such as identifying where people go while online, what people say in chat rooms, and who e-mail is sent to and received from (see http://saxinvestigations.com/).

In addition, as part of the first line of defense, access to sexually explicit web sites can be blocked or at least inhibited in two ways. The first and potentially the best way is to use an ISP that prevents access to sexually explicit web sites. The second way is to use special software that blocks access. While neither of these approaches is failproof, they both have the advantage of making it obvious when a person is starting to lapse into inappropriate online sexual behavior. By making the lapse obvious an opportunity is presented to use coping mechanisms as part of a second line of defense.

Interactive online resources (i.e., bulletin boards and chat) can also assist to reduce anonymity in a somewhat paradoxical way. Individuals often post to bulletin boards under an alias so others don't know their true identity. Yet, they may at the same time become a part of an online community that comes to know them by their alias. The community knows the person is struggling with maintaining abstinence and is there to provide support. As a result of online community involvement, the person's online behavior becomes less anonymous and thus theoretically more inhibited.

The use of bulletin boards, chat, and online 12-step meetings can also be part of the second line of defense. Once a person recognizes that he or she has started to lapse, a preestablished plan can be commenced to use specific interactive online resources. For example, while searching for a work-related topic a patient with a relapse prevention plan sees a link that goes to a web site with sexual content. He thinks to himself, "Gee, where did that come from, it must've slipped through the filter." However, because a plan is in place he also thinks, "I feel like seeing where that link goes, but I'm not going to go there, I'm going to go to my online bulletin board support group instead and tell them about my day, like I said I would in my last therapy session."

As part of the second line of defense, to assist with maintenance of abstinence, conditioning effects can be countered. To achieve this, the conditioned response of sexual arousal to the use of the computer needs to be extinguished. The response will be extinguished when there has been a period of time and Internet use in which no sexual stimulation occurs while using the computer. Breaking the connection of sexual arousal and computer use may be facilitated by strategies that involve only using the computer in places where sexual activity would be undesirable such as libraries, coffee shops, and public work areas. This is similar to the approach described by Young (1999) termed "practice the opposite." The goal of this approach is to have patients disrupt their usual routine and establish new patterns of online behavior in an effort to break their habit.

For some individuals who are severely compulsive even going online in public places may not inhibit the online sexual behavior. In such situations it may be necessary to arrange therapy sessions that include directed nonsexual Internet use. Over time, with the aid of software and ISPs that block pornography access, online computer use in private settings can be initiated. When this transition to private computer use is made, it is important that the individual is familiar with warning signs that precede lapse and have specific coping strategies ready if those signs appear.

In addition to removing the conditioned sexual response, it is also important to address the reinforcement value of the online sexual behavior. The sexual behavior is reinforced because it provides for pleasurable physical sensation, release of sexual energy, and because it is associated with temporary relief from dysphoric emotional states. Thus, to reduce the power of the online sexual experience it is necessary to help patients develop healthy sexuality and also help relieve and resolve emotional distress. This aspect of treatment should include the standard psychotherapeutic and medical approaches warranted for any underlying disorder. As noted by Cooper, Putnam et al. (1999), individuals who engage in online sexual behavior as a way of coping with depression or stress are particularly at risk.

CAPITALIZING ON THE TRIPLE-A ENGINE AND BEHAVIORAL FACTORS IN TREATMENT

Anonymity, accessibility, affordability, and behavioral conditioning have been identified as factors that increase individuals' vulnerability to sexual compulsivity online. These same factors can be utilized to facilitate effective treatment. The following suggestions address how clinicians might use these factors to improve on and augment traditional therapeutic approaches. These strategies are especially appropriate for this population because they are generally computer savvy and will need little or no technological assistance. For specific links to online resources see Cooper et al. (1999).

Contact

Before treatment can occur, contact must be made with an appropriately trained mental health professional. Individuals with stigmatizing conditions, such as sexual addiction, are often reluctant to seek treatment because of shame and fear of being identified. Because of anonymity, individuals may feel free to search online for treatment information and possible providers before they are actually ready to meet or talk to a clinician. Thus, anonymity makes information about starting therapy more available because of the ease of access to it and because emotional barriers are reduced. Also, as a result of improved access to information, therapy becomes more approachable.

Clinicians with web sites benefit from increased exposure to the community and the ability to easily communicate information about their qualifications and areas of expertise. As a result, clinicians can experience an increase in the number, and appropriateness, of referrals. Potential patients benefit because they have the opportunity to learn about treatment providers and make more informed decisions about whom to contact. To facilitate ease of access, clinicians may provide the opportunity for individuals to contact them by e-mail to inquire about services and fees. Clinicians are advised to be cautious and to clearly define how, when, and for what purpose e-mail will be used due to boundary issues. This is particularly true if there are salient boundary issues such as when working with patients with some of the personality disorders. In addition, when offering e-mail contact clinicians may want to provide the following disclaimers regarding the nature of the contact:

1. E-mail contact will be exclusively for the purpose of gathering information and it does not comprise an agreement to establish a therapeutic relationship.
2. The confidentiality of e-mail cannot be guaranteed, but in an effort to keep e-mail as secure as possible it needs to be encrypted. If the patient does not have encryption capabilities, it is suggested that further contact be exclusively by telephone or in person.

It is also recommended that all e-mail contacts with patients be printed and placed in a hardcopy file for future reference. Alternative forms of contact, such as telephone number with posted office hours should also be posted at the web site.

Assessment

The Internet as an educational medium allows for some degree of self-assessment by giving people access to information about symptoms of sex addiction and how they can be manifested in relation to online behavior. As provided in Cooper, Putnam et al. (1999) there are a number of online resources where people can find information about sexual addiction. For example, see the Online Sexual Addiction Questionnaire (http://onlinesexaddict.org/osaq.html), a heuristic tool developed by Putnam (1997a). This information can be helpful to individuals concerned about their own behavior, as well as to family and friends.

Mental health treatment begins with assessment. Treatment of online sexual addiction and compulsivity requires that a thorough psychological, social, and sexual assessment be completed. A discussion of the many factors that need to be assessed is beyond the scope of this article; for additional information on assessment please see Cooper, Putnam et al. (1999).

Typically assessment is done by interview and the use of questionnaires and psychological tests. Online technologies may be used expedite the assessment process and possibly allow for greater disclosure of sensitive information, such as past sexual abuse and trauma. Practical benefits to having patients participate in assessment online include office time and space not being required for completion of questionnaires, questionnaires not being "forgotten" at home, and historical information can be available prior to meeting the patient.

One strategy to assist with information gathering is to create questionnaire forms on web pages. These forms, when completed, may be sent directly to the e-mail address of the clinician. It is suggested that these forms be sent through what is know as a "secure sever" in an effort to keep the information confidential. Any forms that would otherwise be completed in the office (e.g., general information and psychosocial history) could potentially be completed online and sent to the clinician's e-mail address. Two areas that may be particularly beneficial to assess via online questionnaires are sexual history and current pattern of sexual behavior. Assessing these areas online takes advantage of the tendency for people to communicate in the Internet environment with greater disclosure and less restraint in the expression of emotional material. The shame of disclosing intimate sexual details may be eclipsed because the patient is not face to face with a clinician or sitting in a waiting room concerned about being seen. Further, in the case of online sexual addiction, the clinician has the ability to assess the behavior of concern where it is taking place. Assessing the behavior online interjects treatment into an arena where the addict typically would be focused on acting out. This approach can assist with interrupting the pattern of acting out and countering the conditioning effects described earlier.

Clinicians can either pay people to turn their questionnaires into online forms or learn to do it themselves. Computer-savvy clinicians with web sites can learn to create their own forms relatively easily and quickly by adapting web-based programs that are usually available for no additional charge from companies that host web sites. In addition, as online assessment becomes more pervasive, services will likely arise to provide clinicians with additional web-based assessment tools. It is important to note that providing patient confidentiality is the responsibility of mental health professionals and assuring security in the use of forms is a legal as well as ethical requirement.

Treatment

There are a number of ways online resources can augment therapy because they are more accessible, affordable, and allow for greater anonymity than traditional resources. Traditional support resources, such as 12-step meetings, are not always accessible for a variety of reasons. Individuals may not be able to get to meetings due to distance (i.e., live in small towns or rural communities), disability, or concerns regarding anonymity. Many may not attend meetings due to concerns over being embarrassed or identified, which may be especially true for those in high-profile public positions. On the Internet, however, these concerns are either completely resolved or minimized.

In deciding how to use web resources in treatment it is useful to consider both the patient's point in recovery and the types of resources available. Some online exercises will be particularly useful in the early stages of recovery when it is necessary to break through denial and help the patient gain insight, whereas other online activities may be particularly helpful over time as a form of support. The following discussion on the use of online resources to augment therapy is organized in relation to (a) opportunities for insight and support, (b) assistance with education, and (c) homework assignments.

One of the more interesting and powerful opportunities for insight online comes from having access to the stories of other people who are going through or have gone through the same struggle with sexual compulsivity. These stories are available in bulletin board postings and in chat rooms on recovery-oriented web sites. Reading these stories helps people to feel less isolated with their problem and may assist them in breaking through denial. Many end up seeking face-to-face help as a result of the process. It is not unusual for a person to go to a bulletin board and post "I'm not sure I have a problem, but I can't stop doing . . . " In response, another person will reply how it was similar for them and suggest the individual seek therapy or go to a 12-step meeting. Another useful aspect of these forums is the opportunity for sex addicts and partners of sex addicts to gain insight into each other's behavior. Sex addicts have the opportunity to hear what it is like for someone to have their partner exclude them and seek sexual gratification online. Because someone else's partner is telling the story, and not their own, they are often less defensive and better able to hear the story that is being told. Thus, participating in web-based, recovery-oriented communities may assist individuals to develop greater empathy and break through denial.

In the later stages of treatment individuals may use online support groups as a resource to assist in maintaining abstinence. Online groups may develop a history with regular members which allows for accountability to the group, a reduction in isolation, and support in times of need. By regularly participating in online communities via chat-based, 12-step meetings, bulletin board support groups, and e-mail groups, individuals get to know and become known by others and develop an online support system. Thus, regular participation in such a group may serve to help prevent relapse by assisting with everyday coping and in particular with coping in times of crisis.

Outside of therapy, education about sexual addiction is traditionally provided to patients through articles and books, support group meetings, and workshops or classrooms. Now these resources are available online. The advantage of online resources is that they are more accessible than they traditionally have been because of physical location, cost, scheduling, and, probably most important, fear of embarrassment. Articles and books on sexual addiction may be obtained online at any time of day, from any location, and without the purchaser feeling self-conscious or, worse, completely inhibited, as might occur in a library or bookstore. Further, classes that teach about the signs and symptoms of sexual addiction and introduce treatment approaches are beginning to be available (see http://onlinesexaddict.org/course.html). In addition, there are numerous web sites and forums that provide useful information on other mental disorders that can be associated with sexual addiction.

The web also provides opportunities for new and creative homework assignments, as well as improved ways to complete traditional assignments. New opportunities include having the patient engage in specific activities using the resources already mentioned. A few examples include having patients visit clinician-designated web sites and report back on what was learned, read posts on a bulletin board written by people with problems similar to them or their spouse, anonymously post their story on a bulletin board, participate in an online 12-step meeting, and take an online class about sexual addiction. New ways of completing old tasks include having patients use online forms to complete written exercises. Written exercises can be used as a method of assessment to track progress throughout therapy and as a way to facilitate processing of therapeutic issues. For example, online exercises can be designed to help patients recognize how their behavior has been harmful and why they continued to engage in it as well as to develop new coping strategies. The online forms can also have a quasi-interactive component in which the patient is first directed to engage in various online activities and then report his or her experience doing so on the form. This way using the form assists the individual in processing his or her experience in real time and the therapist gains additional access to an experience occurring outside of therapy.

It is recommended that clinicians do not attempt to moderate support groups online but rather work with patients using self-help forums like 12-step groups as adjuncts to treatment. Clinicians who attempt to run online text-based groups as therapy groups run the risk of violating state laws and ethics codes. Practicing outside of the state one is licensed in is illegal and providing services in a modality one has not been trained in is unethical. Practitioners are advised to be aware of their state licensing laws and to obtain malpractice insurance for every state in which they practice.

BEHAVIORAL TELEHEALTH

People who are seeking help with their out-of-control online sexual behavior will soon find they can receive therapeutic assistance via an area known as *Behavioral Telehealth*. Behavioral Telehealth is a specialty within an emerging area known as Telehealth. Telehealth involves using technology to provide medical and psychological services (Bashshur, 1997; Council on Competitiveness, 1996; DeLeon, Sammons, Frank, & VandenBos, in press) and been defined as "the use of telecommunications and information technology to provide access to health assessment, diagnosis, intervention, consultation, supervision, education, and information across distance" (Nickelson, 1998b, p. 527). Technologies used to provide Telehealth services include traditional telephone, videophones, and interactive video on the Internet

Behavioral Telehealth may be used to provide patient education, assessment, diagnosis, and treatment, including crisis intervention, psychotherapy, and prescription of psychotropic medications (Administrative Rules of Montana, 1995; DeLeon, Folen, Jennings, & Willis, 1991; DeLeon & Wiggins, 1996; McCarthy, Kulakowski, & Kenfield, 1994; Nickelson, 1998c; Stamm, 1995, 1998). Currently Behavioral Telehealth represents over 20% of Telehealth practice in the United States (DeLeon et al., in press) and is the fastest growing area of Telehealth (D. Puskin, personal communication, April 22, 1999). Behavioral Telehealth services have typically been delivered by psychiatrists and nurse practitioners; however, the opportunity now exists for other mental health professionals to start offering Telehealth services.

Videoconferencing is becoming the primary technology being used for psychotherapy in Behavioral Telehealth programs (Baer, Cukor, Jenike, Leahy, O'Laughlen, & Coyle, 1995; Cukor, Baer, Willis, Leahy, O'Laughlen, Murphy, Withers, & Martin, 1998; Huston & Burton, 1997; Glueckauf et al., 1998; Jerome, 1986, 1993; Sampson, Kolodinsky, & Greeno, 1997; Troster, Paolo, Glatt, Hubble, & Koller, 1995). The positive effect of interactive video upon the offline therapeutic alliance has been demonstrated by a number of researchers (Baigent, Bond, Kalucy, Yellowlees, Ben-Torin, Kavanagh, & Lloyd, 1997; Ball, McLaren, Summerfield, Lipsedge, & Watson, 1995; Ghosh, McLaren, & Watson, 1997; Jerome, 1993; McLaren, Blunder, Lipsedge, & Summerfield, 1996; Montani, Billaud, Tyrell, & Fluchaire, 1997). Early research indicates that videoconferencing " . . . works well for group therapy as well as individual consults" (Department of Commerce, 1997, p. 19). Because of the opportunities that exist, videoconferencing is now being integrated into professional psychological training at graduate and postgraduate levels (J. Albino, personal communication, January 19, 1999; R. Levant, personal communication, January 19, 1999; Sampson, Kolodinsky, & Greeno, 1997). Although these early studies have been conducted offline, using videophones or more expensive videoconferencing equipment, the opportunities are great for researchers who want to explore videoconferencing as a tool for treatment outreach with sexually compulsive individuals over the Internet

Videoconferencing services of adequate speed and resolution are beginning to be available for psychotherapists to use over the Internet Using video with sexually compulsive patients has a distinct advantage over text-based interaction, such as exists with e-mail or chat. When text-based interaction alone is provided to patients whose disorder revolves around anonymity, it can support their propensity toward operating as an unknown, unseen, unheard, and disembodied entity. The use of video resolves many of the issues because the participants are seen and heard and it allows the therapist to attend to verbal and nonverbal cues. While those engaged in compulsive online sexual behavior are likely to be reluctant to give up their anonymity, it will probably be easier for them to first see a therapist while seated at their computer than to make an appointment and walk in to someone's office. Thus, it appears that at least in the initial stages of treatment Behavioral Telehealth may be especially useful with people with compulsive online sexual behavior because it may allow for earlier intervention and possibly intervention with people who would not otherwise obtain treatment.

As with traditional therapy, it behooves practitioners to complete a thorough assessment and to obtain as much real-life experience of the patient as possible through videoconferencing. In addition, it is important for the clinician to be aware of backup services in the patient's community so that crises that require face-to-face contact can be managed. Once assessment has been completed, backup plans have been determined, and treatment has been initiated, the practitioner may explore creative ways to make use of the technology to improve treatment in ways previously unavailable. For example, in providing psychotherapy via videoconferencing with a sexually compulsive patient, the practitioner can benefit from the "window into the patient's home" (W. Karp, personal communication, November 19, 1999). Because the clinician can see the patient's environment he or she can learn much more about the patient than might be experienced in a face-to-face office visit. Lifestyle, dress, organization, and many other cues given by the patient's environment can be discussed and brought into the treatment by the therapist, as is needed to help the patient reach therapeutic goals. In addition, when appropriate, treatment can be expanded to include the spouse and/or family members to deal with the secretiveness of the disorder and its repercussions. Videoconferencing provides an increased capacity for family interaction that is unprecedented and may allow for system-based therapeutic opportunities that previously were not possible (Karp, Bogan, Mohanty, & Karp, 1999).

ETHICAL, LEGAL, AND REGULATORY ISSUES:
LOOK BEFORE YOU LEAP

A variety of professionals are delivering information using the Internet (Frisse, Kelly, & Mercalfe, 1994; Rusovick & Warner, 1998; Sleek, 1997). Yet, despite the growth of Telehealth and media attention regarding "online psychotherapy, " remarkably few licensed professionals are offering psychotherapy via e-mail and chat rooms on the Internet (Maheu & Gordon, 2000). Concerns regarding the practice of psychotherapy online include variable quality of patient information, lack of credentialing and accountability of professionals, and consumer's inability to determine the credentials of professionals who offer psychotherapy online. The lack of patient protection alternatives available to consumers has also been noted (Murry, 1998; Health on the Net, 1998). Further, a particular concern related to offering treatment to sexually compulsive individuals online is the difficulty of accurately diagnosing and treating patients, especially when e-mail or chat rooms are used. For example, comorbid substance abuse and dependence may be easier for patients to conceal when they are not met within a face-to-face environment. In addition, particular caution and safeguards need to be put in place to deal with patients who could become suicidal or homicidal. Thus, it is important for clinicians to become familiar with the resources available in the communities of the people they serve. Detecting critical conditions such as substance use and suicidality is necessary for proper treatment to occur, and the greater the number of technological and face-to-face accesses to obtaining such information, the greater the chance of successful treatment.

Ethics, credentialing, and licensing boards are being challenged by the complexities of Telehealth. Several groups including the World Health Organization, various branches of the U.S. government (DHHS, 1997a, b; IOM, 1996; Ryboski, 1998; U.S. Congress, 1995) and professional associations such as the American Medical Health Informatics Management Association (Brandt, 1996), the American Medical Informatics Association (Kane & Sands, 1998), the National Council of State Boards of Nursing (1998) and the National Board for Certified Counselors (1998) are providing suggestions and leadership toward the ethical guidelines.

One of the most pressing issues needing examination is the electronic patient record. Centralized electronic medical records are being developed into a single, multiuser database in the United States (Computer-based Patient Record Institute, 1999). Theoreticians and researchers in psychology (Maheu, 1998; Maheu, Whitten, & Allen, 2000; Maheu, Callan, & Nagy, in press; Nickelson, 1998b; Stamm, 1998) and medicine (Carroll, Wright, & Zakoworotny, 1998; Spielberg, 1998; Waller & Alcantara, 1998) as well as professionals from other countries (Mitka, 1998) are discussing the protection of patient information. The importance of protecting the confidentiality of medical records is of particular import to patients who seek treatment for sexual disorders since a breach in confidentiality could result in severe repercussions for them. Thus, due diligence on the part of practitioners is crucial with respect to the medical records of their sexually compulsive patients.

A number of other practice concerns arise when practitioners develop behavioral health care practices using any form of technology. Concerns include malpractice coverage and liabilities (Office of Technology Assessment, 1995), ramifications of practicing outside the "standard of care," emergency backup, storage of videotapes of procedures, and proper documentation of services delivered (Brandt & Carpenter, 1999). Particularly important when attempting to treat minors who seek treatment for sexual compulsivity online are the issues of parental consent to treatment and laws related to patient rights concerning their psychological record (California Healthline, 1999).

Reimbursement for services rendered can also be an issue. Models are being developed that include billing third party carriers and alternatively having patients pay fees monthly, upfront, by credit card, on the first of every month. In California, for example, legislation has already been enacted that prohibits the addition of surcharges for equipment when delivering services through specified Telehealth technologies, and the cost of transmission and equipment is not considered a reimbursable expense (Telemedicine Act, 1996). Legal issues regarding reimbursement are complex and vary from state to state. Controversy reigns, and rights to reimbursement are being fought in fierce turf wars. For example, despite the 1999 federal budget requirement that psychologists and social workers be reimbursed for Telehealth services, they have now been excluded as recipients of such benefits (Cepelewicz, 1998; Medicare program, 1988; Nickelson, 1998a; Payment for Teleconsultations, 1998; Rabasca, 1999).

Ethical, legal, and regulatory issues are unresolved and much is yet to be determined. Practitioners are cautioned to be thorough when preparing to offer services on the web and via Behavioral Telehealth technology. It is prudent to do the following before proceeding: (a) develop a comprehensive risk management program that includes a thorough patient consent form, (b) obtain written verification of malpractice coverage for all technology-based services for each state within which you practice, (c) seek guidance and approval of activities from local, state, and national ethics and licensing boards, (d) be aware of your state laws and those of the patients you choose to treat, and (e) be able to quickly access backup emergency services in all geographical areas within which you treat (Maheu, 1999).

CONCLUSION

As a result of technology, we are seeing new variations of sexual addiction and compulsivity. It appears that people who were not sexually compulsive in the past now have developed problems due to a combination of their particular personal vulnerabilities and factors unique to the online environment. These individuals are searching for help for their compulsive sexuality online, where they are experiencing it. As a result, clinicians are now faced with the opportunity and challenge to meet these people where they are in order to facilitate their treatment. The task of incorporating online resources into treatment and providing therapy using Behavioral Telehealth technologies may be daunting, especially to clinicians unfamiliar with the technology. However, the potential for these technologies being helpful to those in need of treatment, and rewarding for the clinicians interested in treating them, makes it a task worthy of pursuit.

It is the responsibility of the mental health professional to uphold legal and ethical mandates while developing this new area of practice. In considering the development of resources and a psychotherapeutic model we must identify which delivery systems will best suit each patient with consideration of diagnosis and stage in the treatment process. An individually tailored combination of e-mail, interactive video, and face-to-face treatment, integrated with the use of online education and group social support, could be optimal for the treatment of sexually compulsive individuals. This approach provides patients with greater access to services and clinicians with greater access to information about their patients. Using online resources can also facilitate a more comprehensive treatment program, especially for those reluctant or unable to attend regular therapy sessions.

REFERENCES

Administrative Rules of Montana. (1995). Statutes and Rules Relating to Psychologists. §8.52.606 (2).

Anderson, N., & Coleman, E. (1991). Childhood abuse and family sexual attitudes in sexually compulsive males: A comparison of three clinical groups. *American Journal of Preventive Psychiatry and Neurology, 3,* 8–15.

Baer, L., Cukor, P., Jenike, M., Leahy, B., O'Laughlen, J., & Coyle, J. (1995). Pilot studies of telemedicine for patients with obsessive compulsive disorder. *American Journal of Psychiatry, 152,* 1383–1385.

Baigent, M. F., Bond, M. J., Kalucy, R. S., Yellowlees, P. M., Ben-Tovim, D. I., Kavanagh, S. J., & Lloyd, C. J. (1997). Telepsychiatry: 'Tele' yes, but what about the 'psychiatry'? *Journal of Telemedicine and Telecare, 3* (Supplement 1), 3–5.

Ball, C. J., McLaren, P. M., Summerfield, A. B., Lipsedge, M. S., & Watson, J. P. (1995). A comparison of communication modes in adult psychiatry. *Journal of Telehealth and Telecare, 1,* 22–26.

Bashshur, R. L. (1997). Telemedicine and the health care system. In R. L. Bashshur, J. H. Sanders, & G. W. Shannon (Eds.), *Telemedicine—Theory and practice* (pp. 5-35). Springfield, IL: Charles C Thomas.

Bradford, J. (1997). Medical interventions in sexual deviance. In D. R. Laws & W O'Donohue (Eds.), *Sexual deviance: Theory, assessment, and treatment* (pp. 449–464). New York: The Guilford Press.

Brandt, M. D. (1996). Practice guidelines for managing health information. *American Health Informatics Management Association Practice Brief* (Document 406).

Brandt, M. & Carpenter, J. (1999, January). Patient photography, videotaping, and other imaging (Updated). *AMIHA Practice Brief* [Online]. Available: http://www.ahima.org/publications/2a/pract.brief.0199b.html

California Healthline. (1999, April 21). Medical privacy: Agreement, but a long way to go [Online]. Available: http://www.chcf.org/press/viewpress.cfm?itemID=362

Carnes, P. (1991). *Don't call it love: Recovery from sexual addiction.* New York: Bantam Books.

Carnes, P. (1993). Addiction and post-traumatic stress: The convergence of victims' realities. *Treating Abuse Today, 3*(13), 5–11.

Carroll, E. T., Wright, S., & Zakoworotny, C. (1998). Securely implementing remote access within health information management. *Journal of American Health Information Management Association, 69*(3), 46–49.

Cepelewicz, B. (1998, October 8). *Telemedicine and strategies to minimize risks of liability.* Paper presented at the Telemedicine National Conference on Legal and Policy Developments, Washington, DC.

Coleman, E. (1992). Is your patient suffering from compulsive sexual behavior? *Psychiatric Annals, 22*(6), 320–325.

Computer-based Patient Record Institute. (1999). *CPRI Toolkit: Managing information security in health care.* Bethesda, MD: Author.

Cooper, A. (1998). Sexuality and the Internet: Surfing into the new millennium. *CyberPsychology & Behavior, 1,* 187–193.

Cooper, A., Delmonico, D., & Burg, R. (2000). Cybersex users, abusers, compulsives: New findings and implications. *Sexual Addiction & Compulsivity, 7,* 5–29.

Cooper, A., Putnam, D. E., Planchon, L. A., & Boies, S. C. (1999). Online sexual compulsivity: Getting tangled in the net *Sexual Addiction & Compulsivity, 6,* 79–104.

Cooper, A., Scherer, C. R., Boies, S. C., & Gordon, B. L. (1999). Sexuality on the Internet: From sexual exploration to pathological expression. *Professional Psychology, 30*(2), 154–164.

Council on Competitiveness. (1996). *Highway to health: Transforming U. S. health care in the information age.* Washington, DC.

Cukor, P., Baer, L., Willis, B. S., Leahy, L., O'Laughlen, J., Murphy, M. E., Withers, M., and Martin, E. (1998). Use of videophones and low-cost standard telephone lines to provide a social presence in telepsychiatry. *Telemedicine Journal, 4*(4), 313–321.

Cutter, F. (1996). Virtual psychotherapy? *Psychnews International, Section B, 1* (3). [Online]. Available: http://mentalhelp.net/pni/pni13b.htm

DeLeon, P. H., Folen, R. A., Jennings, F. L., & Willis, D. J. (1991). The case for prescription privileges: A logical evolution of professional practice [Special issue: Child psychopharmacology]. *Journal of Clinical Child Psychology, 20,* 254–267.

DeLeon, P. H., VandenBos, G. R., Sammons, M. T., & Frank, R. G. (1998). Changing health care environment in the United States: Steadily evolving into the 21st century. In A. S. Bellack & M. Hersen (Series Eds.) and A. N. Wiens (Vol. Ed.), *Comprehensive clinical psychology:* (Vol. 2) *Professional issues* (1st ed., pp. 393–401). Great Britain: Elsevier Science.

DeLeon, P. H., & Wiggins, J. G. (1996). Prescription privileges for psychologists. *American Psychologist, 51,* 225–229.

Delmonico, D. L. (1997). Cybersex: High tech sex addiction. *Sexual Addiction and Compulsivity, 4*(2), 159–167.

Department of Commerce. (1997). Telemedicine Report to Congress. [Online]. Available: http://www.ntia.doc.gov/reports/telemed/index.htm

Earle, R. H., & Earle, M. R. (1995). *Sex addiction: Case studies and management.* New York: Brunner/Mazel.

Frisse, M., Kelly, E., & Mercalfe, E. (1994). An Internet primer: Resources and responsibilities. *Acad Med, 69*(1), 20–24.

Ghosh, G. J., McLaren, P. M., & Watson, J. P. (1997). Evaluating the alliance in videolink teletherapy. *Journal of Telemedicine and Telecare, 3*(Suppl. 1), 33–35.

Glueckauf, R., Whitton, J., Baxter, J., Kain, J., Vogelgesang, S., Hudson, M., Dustin Wright, D., Jared, B., Falco, M. (1998). Videocounseling for families of rural teens with epilepsy—Project update. *Telehealth News [Online Serial], 1*(4), 1–2. [Online]. Available: http://telehealth.net/telehealth/newslettr_4a.html

Greenfield, D. N. (in press). *Virtual addiction: Help for netheads, cyberfreaks, and those who love them.* Oakland, CA: New Harbinger Publications.

Grubin, D., & Mason, D. (1997). Medical models of sexual deviance. In D. R. Laws & W. O'Donohue (Eds.), *Sexual deviance: Theory, assessment, and treatment* (pp. 434–448). New York: The Guilford Press.

Hapgood, F. (1996). Sex Sells, Inc. *Technology, 4,* 45–51.

Health on the Net Foundation Code of Conduct for Medical and Health Web Sites. (1998). [HONcode principles]. [Online]. Available: http://www.hon.ch/HONcode/Conduct.html

Huston, J. L., & Burton, D. C. (1997). Patient satisfaction with multispecialty interactive teleconsultations. *Journal of Telemedicine and Telecare, 3*(4), 205–208.

Institute of Medicine (IOM). (1996). *Telemedicine: A guide to assessing telecommunications in health care,* M. J. Field (Ed.). Washington, DC: National Academy Press.

Jerome, L. (1986). Telepsychiatry. *Canadian Journal of Psychiatry, 31,* 489.

Jerome, L. (1993). Assessment by telemedicine. *Hospital and Community Psychiatry, 44,* 81-83.

Junginger, J. (1997). Fetishism: Assessment and treatment. In D. R. Laws & W. O'Donohue (Eds.), *Sexual deviance: Theory, assessment, and treatment* (pp. 92–110). New York: The Guilford Press.

Kafka, M., & Prentky, R. (1992). Fluoxetine treatment of nonparaphilic sexual addictions and paraphilias in men. *Journal of Clinical Psychiatry, 53,* 351–358.

Kane, B., & Sands, D. (1998). Guidelines for the clinical use of electronic mail with patients. Internet Working Group, Task Force on Guidelines for the use of Clinic-Patient Electronic Mail. *Journal of the American Medical Informatics Association, 5,* 104–111.

Karp, W. B., Bogan, E., Mohanty, B. V., & Karp, N. V. (1999, March). The use of telehealth videoconferencing technology to support the delivery of early intervention services into natural environments. Article submitted for publication in *Journal Develop Behavioral Pediatrics.*

Leiblum, S. R. (1997). Sex and the net: Clinical implications. *Journal of Sex Education and Therapy, 22*(1), 21–27.

Maheu, M. (1997). Will online services for consumer self-help improve behavioral healthcare? *Behavioral Healthcare Tomorrow Journal, 6*(6).

Maheu, M. (1998). Telehealth - A call to action. American Association of Behavior Therapists. *The Behavior Therapist, 21*(6).

Maheu, M. (1999). Risk management in the re-tooling of healthcare. *TelehealthNet* [Online]. Available: http://telehealth.net/articles/riskman3.html

Maheu, M., Callan, J., & Nagy, T. (in press). Call to Action: Ethical and legal issues for Behavioral Telehealth including online psychological services. In S. Bucky (Ed.), *Comprehensive textbook of ethics and law on the practice of psychology.* New York: Plenum Publishers.

Maheu, M., & Gordon, B. (1999). *Psychotherapy on the Internet: Legal, ethical and practice issues.* Manuscript submitted for publication.

Maheu, M., Whitten, & Allen, A. (2000). *eHealth, telemedicine and telehealth: A comprehensive guide to program start-up and success.* San Francisco: Jossey-Bass.

McCarthy, P., Kulakowski, D., & Kenfield, J. A. (1994). Clinical supervision practices of licensed psychologists. *Professional Psychology: Research & Practice, 25,* 177–181.

McLaren, P. M., Blunden, J., Lipsedge, M. L., & Summerfield, A. B. (1996). Telepsychiatry in an inner-city community psychiatric service. *Journal of Telemedicine and Telecare, 2,* 57–59.

Medicare program. (1998). Scope of Medicare benefits and application of the outpatient mental health treatment limitation to clinical psychologist and clinical social worker services, 63 Fed. Reg. 21010.

Mitka, M. (1998). Developing countries find telemedicine forges links to more care and research. *The Journal of the American Medical Association, 280*(15), 1295–1296.

Montani, C., Billaud, N., Tyrrell, J., & Fluchaire, I. (1997). Psychological impact of a remote psychometric consultation with hospitalized elderly people. *Journal of Telemedicine and Telecare, 3,* 140–145.

Murry, B. (1998, March). Data smog: Newest culprit in brain drain. *APA Monitor, 29.* [Online]. Available: http://www.apa.org/monitor/mar98/smog.html

National Board for Certified Counselors. (1998). Standards for the Ethical Practice of WebCounseling. [Online]. Available: http://www.nbcc.org/ethics/wcstandards.htm

National Council of State Boards of Nursing. (1998, April). Boards of nursing approve proposed language for an interstate compact for a mutual recognition model for nursing regulation. *Communique,* 1–4.

Nickelson, D. (1997). Politics & policy. *TelehealthNews, 1*(4), 1–2. [Online].

Nickelson, D. (1998a). Telehealth: Rural Medicare reimbursement, reduced telecom rates and grant funding opportunities, *Rural Health Bulletin, 4*(1). [Online]. Available: http://www.apa.org/rural/rhb98.html#art3

Nickelson, D. (1998b). Telehealth and the evolving health care system: Strategic opportunities for professional psychology. *Professional Psychology: Research and Practice, 29*(6), 527–535.

Office of Technology Assessment. (1995, September). Bringing health care online: The role of information technologies, OTA-ITC-624. Washington, DC: U.S. Government Printing Office. [Online]. Available: http://www.wws.princeton.edu/cgi-bin/byteserv.prl/~ota/disk1/1995/9507/9507.PDF

Payment for Teleconsultations in Rural Health Professional Shortage Areas. (1998). 63 Fed. Reg. 58879.

Putnam, D. E. (1997a). *Online Sexual Addiction Questionnaire.* [Online]. Available: http://onlinesexaddict.com/osaq.html

Putnam, D. E. (1997b). Module 4 - Behavioral theory and the cycle of addiction.

Online Sexual Addiction Course. [Online]. Available: http://onlinesexaddict.com/course/module4.html

Putnam, D. E. (1998, March). Advances in distance learning. In B. L. Gordon (Chair), *Issues and opportunities in behavioral telehealth*. Symposium presented at the annual meeting of the California Psychological Association, Pasadena, California.

Putnam, D. E. (1999, March). Assessment and treatment of online sexual addiction. In D. E. Putnam (Chair), *Cybersex: Psychological assessment, treatment, and ethical issues*. Symposium presented at the annual meeting of the California Psychological Association, San Diego, California.

Rabasca, L. (1999, February). HCFA rejects telehealth payment for psychologists. *APA Monitor,* p. 27.

Rickards, S., & Laaser, M. (1999). Sexual acting-out in borderline women: Impulsive self-destructiveness or sexual addiction/compulsivity. *Sexual Addiction & Compulsivity, 6*(1), 31–46.

Robinson, D.W. (1999). Sexual addiction as an adaptive response to post-traumatic stress disorder in the African American community. *Sexual Addiction & Compulsivity, 6,* 11–22.

Rusovick, R. M., & Warner, D. J. (1998). The globalization of interventional informatics through Internet mediated distributed medical intelligence. *New Medicine, 2,* 155–161.

Ryboski, L. (1998, July). *National Health Policy Forum: Protecting the confidentiality of health information*. George Washington University, Washington, DC.

Sampson, J., Kolodinsky, R., & Greeno, B. (1997). Counseling on the information highway: Future possibilities and potential problems. *Journal of Counseling and Development, 75*(3), 203–212.

Schwartz, M. (1992). Sexual compulsivity as post-traumatic stress disorder: Treatment perspectives. *Psychiatric Annals, 22,* 333–338.

Sealy, J. R. (1999). Dual and triple diagnoses: Addictions, mental illness, and HIV infection guidelines for outpatient therapists. *Sexual Addiction & Compulsivity, 6*(3), 195–220.

Sleek, S. (1997, August). Providing therapy from a distance. *APA Monitor,* p. 1, 38.

Spielberg, A. R. (1998). On call and online: Sociohistorical, legal, and ethical implications of e-mail for the patient-physician relationship. *The Journal of the American Medical Association, 280,* 1353–1359.

Stamm, B. H. (1995). *Secondary traumatic stress: Self-care issues for clinicians, researchers and educators*. Lutherville, MD: Sidran Press.

Stamm, B. (1998). Clinical applications of Telehealth in mental health care. *Professional Psychology: Research and Practice, 29*(6), 536–542.

Tedesco, A., & Bola, J. R. (1997). A pilot study of the relationship between childhood sexual abuse and compulsive sexual behavior in adults. *Sexual Addiction and Compulsivity, 4*(2), 147–157.

Telemedicine Act. (1996). Cal. Stats. 864. [Online]. Available: http://www.leginfo.ca.gov/pub/95-96/bill/sen/sb_16511700/sb_1665_bill_960925_-chaptered.html

Troster, A., Paolo, A., Glatt, S., Hubble, J., & Koller, W. (1995). Interactive video conferencing in the provision of neuropsychological services to rural areas. *Journal of Community Psychology, 23,* 85–88.

Waller, A., & Alcantara, O. (1998). Ownership of health information in the informa-

tion age. *Journal of American Health Information Management Association,*
    69(3), 28–38.

Whitfield, C. L. (1998). Internal evidence and corroboration of traumatic memories
    of child sexual abuse with addictive disorders. *Sexual Addiction & Compulsivity:*
    The Journal of Treatment and Prevention, 6, 79–104.

Young, K. (1999). Internet addiction: Symptoms, evaluation, and treatment. In L.
    VandeCreek & T. Jackson (Eds.), *Innovations in clinical practice: A source book*
    (Vol. 17; pp. 1–13). Sarasota, FL: Professional Resource Press.

Chapter 6

Should Virtual Sex Be Treated Like Other Sex Addictions?

MARESSA HECHT ORZACK

McLean Hospital, Belmont, Massachusetts, USA

CAROL J. ROSS

Sierra Tucson Inc., Tucson, Arizona, USA

The majority of those addicted to virtual sex who present for outpatient and inpatient treatment usually have more pervasive sexual or other behavioral and/or chemical addictions. Case studies are presented to illustrate typical patients. Treatment recommendations are made for both outpatient and inpatient treatment. Beck Hopelessness Scale test results show a significant improvement in those treated with inpatient modalities. As in treating other sex addictions, imposing limits and enlisting the aid of others works for some cybersex addicts, while others need a period of complete abstinence or to eliminate computer use entirely.

INTRODUCTION

The aim of this article is to illustrate the complexities of treating compulsive Internet sex in both an inpatient and an outpatient setting. Although we are using examples from different institutions, our assessments and our treatment procedures are remarkably similar. Several points need to be stressed. First, the treatment requires a multidisciplinary approach. Our case studies are typical patients addicted to personal use of a computer and the Internet for sexual purposes (cybersex). They meet the criteria for at least one or more comorbid disorders. Shapira (1998) found this true for the majority of his sample.

Second, it is inappropriate in this computer-driven world to ask most patients to abstain from computer use. However, it is important to note that

---

Thanks to David Anderson, Ph.D., for his testing and interpretive skills on the BHS and to Deborah S. Orzack, M.S., for her invaluable editorial help.

Address correspondence to Maressa Hecht Orzack, Ph.D., at McLean Hospital, 115 Mill St., Belmont, MA 02478, USA, or to Carol Ross, MA, CADC, at Sierra Tucson, 39580 S. Lago Del Oro Parkway, Tucson, AZ 85739, USA.

there may be severe cases in which limiting computer use is not enough and periods of abstinence must be recommended. This is particularly true of the inpatient cases.

Third, the treatment model is primarily based on an eating disorder model where patients must be taught to manage their inappropriate computer use for optimal health.

Cooper (2000) states that the Internet entices people to act in ways that they would not normally act. Orzack (1998, 1999) compiled a list of symptoms specific to computer addiction (Table 1). This is based on the criteria for pathological gambling as presented in the *Diagnostic and Statistical Manual of Mental Disorders* (APA, 1994). The National Council on Sexual Addiction and Compulsivity describes sexual addiction as "persistent and escalating patterns of sexual behavior acted out despite increasing negative consequences to self and others" (Schneider, 1991). Goodman (1998) identifies criteria for sexual addiction (see Table 2), an earlier version of which is also based on the criteria for pathological gambling.

The assessment of sexual addiction shows that it is not necessarily the frequency or kind of behavior, but the loss of control, or compulsivity and negative consequences, that indicate addiction. However, in their study of 9,265 Internet users, Cooper et al. (2000) found that the nonsexually compulsive respondents (83.5%), the moderately sexually compulsive respondents (10.9%), and the sexually compulsive respondents (4.6%) spent about 1 to 10 hours per week pursuing online sexual material, while the "cybersex compulsive" respondents (1%), spent an average of 10 to 25 hours per week pursuing sex online. While those in the sexually compulsive group used online sex as part of their sexually compulsive behaviors, those in the cybersex

---

TABLE 1. Computer/Internet Addiction Disorder

Persistent and recurrent misuse of the computer is indicated by at least five of the following:

1. Experiences pleasure, gratification, or relief while engaged in computer activities.
2. Preoccupation with computer activity, including thinking about the experience, making plans to return to the computer, surfing the web, having the newest and fastest hardware.
3. Needing to spend more and more time or money on computer activities to change mood.
4. Failure of repeated efforts to control these activities.
5. Restlessness, irritability, or other dysphoric moods such as increase in tension when not engaged in computer activities.
6. Need to return to these activities to escape problems or relieve dysphoric mood.
7. Neglect of social, familial, educational, or work obligations.
8. Lying to family members, therapists, and others about the extent of time spent on the computer.
9. Actual or threatened loss of significant relationships, job, financial stability, or educational opportunity because of computer usage.
10. Show physical signs, such as carpal tunnel syndrome, backaches, dry eyes, migraines, headaches, neglect of personal hygiene or eating irregularities.
11. Changes in sleep patterns.

Computer misuse is not better accounted for by OCD or a manic episode.

Maressa Hecht Orzack, Ph.D., August 1999

TABLE 2. Definition of Sexual Addiction

Sexual Addiction: A maladaptive pattern of sexual behavior, leading to clinically significant impairment or distress, as manifested by three (or more) of the following, occurring at any time in the same 12-month period:

(1) tolerance as defined by either of the following:
  (a) a need for markedly increased amount or intensity of the sexual behavior to achieve the desired effect
  (b) markedly diminished effect with continued involvement in the sexual behavior at the same level of intensity

(2) withdrawal, as manifested by either of the following:
  (a) characteristic psychophysiological withdrawal syndrome of physiologically described changes and/or psychologically described changes upon discontinuation of the sexual behavior
  (b) the same (or a closely related) sexual behavior is engaged in to relieve or avoid withdrawal symptoms

(3) the sexual behavior is often engaged in over a longer period, in greater quantity, or at a higher level of intensity than was intended

(4) there is a persistent desire or unsuccessful efforts to cut down or control the sexual behavior

(5) a greater deal of time is spent in activities necessary to prepare for the sexual behavior, to engage in the behavior, and to recover from its effects

(6) important social, occupational, or recreational activities are given up or reduced because of the sexual behavior

(7) the psychological problem that is likely to have been caused or exacerbated by sexual behavior continues despite knowledge of its consequences

Note. From "Sexual addiction: The new frontier" by A. Goodman, 1998. *The Counselor,* volume 16, copyright © 1998. Adapted by permission.

compulsive group used online sex as their main sexually compulsive behavior, or their "drug of choice." This supports our experience that most clients (inpatient and outpatient) who use cybersex addictively also display signs and symptoms of more pervasive sexual/behavioral compulsivities. The following case studies represent such arrays of behavior and are similar enough to each other to contrast the difference between inpatient and outpatient treatments.

CASE STUDIES

Inpatient

Jeff was a 38-year-old male who came to inpatient treatment as a result of an intervention after his wife discovered his online romance with another woman. He presented with depressive symptoms and sexual disorder, not otherwise specified.

Jeff came from a very religious family who had high expectations for Jeff's success. Early in his childhood, Jeff found masturbation a secret relief from the pressures of these expectations of perfection. He never got caught and his only consequence was his guilt about his secret self-soothing. When he and a childhood male peer found a soft porn magazine in the outside trash can one day, his secret sexual life took on a new excitement. Not only did it add visual stimulation to his masturbation, but also now another person became part of his secretive sexual life. Feeling innately bad, Jeff felt he could never tell those closest to him, such as his parents, his pastor, or friends, for they already knew Jeff as a high-achieving "good boy."

Jeff's sexual history seemed unremarkable throughout his teen years. Continuing the perfect image, he had a steady girlfriend in high school, whom he kissed and explored physically, without intercourse. In college, he began experimenting with casual dating, various forms of pornography, and intercourse. One of Jeff's sexual relationships was with a woman who became pregnant by him. They decided to get an abortion, a decision that prompted additional guilt and shame. Again, Jeff could not feel safe in confiding to anyone about this, except the female partner. As his internal conflict grew between his expected image and his sexual experiences, Jeff worked ever so much harder to achieve. Upon meeting his future wife, he experienced a sexual life with much less shame. However, during their engagement, he was unfaithful with a former sex partner. It only happened once, so he felt he could keep it a secret from his fiancée and others without costing him the security and stability of his image and his betrothal to a religious and pretty wife.

After their marriage, it seemed to Jeff that the worst was over as far as inner turmoil and shame about his sexual behaviors. However, after the birth of their first child, he felt particularly inadequate in his new role as a father and his wife seemed less interested in sex. He was vulnerable to an emotional affair at work, which began as a friendship and progressed into sexual tension and attraction. Once again Jeff was living a double life that added a familiar level of internal stress for him. Throughout the history of his marriage, he began to use pornography increasingly and masturbation to self-soothe, as his sexual relationship with his wife decreased in frequency.

One night on his way home from a Christian businessmen's meeting, a prostitute approached Jeff as he sat in his car at a stoplight. Without thinking, Jeff invited her into his car. Although Jeff's sexual behavior had escalated to a new level, to him it seemed a safer alternative to a workplace affair and the risk of his wife catching him masturbating to pornography—a behavior she condemned. Jeff continued to see the same prostitute and considered her a friend. When he became ashamed of this behavior, he stopped seeing the prostitute.

Soon thereafter, he began secretly spending time in romantic and sexual chats on the Internet. He also sometimes logged onto sexual web sites. His secret time online began at work when everyone else had gone home. Then, Jeff began coming into work early some mornings to chat online with women. Jeff knew there was a chance of getting caught, but this made his secret online usage even more exciting. At times his fear and shame overcame him and he promised himself he would stop. He began replacing those early morning chats with cable television exercise shows. He justified watching scantily clad women exercise instructors as healthier than what he had been doing, but it was not long before Jeff began sneaking into the family's home office to chat online late at night. Suspicious of his strange moods, his wife began investigating their home computer and found revealing e-mails from his online romantic affair. He had become careless about covering up his tracks at home. What Jeff did not know was that his employer had already become suspicious, based on the workplace computer's log-on history of Jeff's strange times of computer use.

Like most patients who come for inpatient treatment, Jeff had a sexual addiction that he had tried to limit or control for many years by changing from one type of sexual activity to another so that he or others would not see any problem with it. However, online sex sites and chat rooms, compared to other sexual behaviors, are easier to detect, trace, and even accidentally discover by wives, children, coworkers, and employers.

Outpatient

George is a 38-year-old married man who was referred to the clinic for obsessive use of pornography. He presented with depression and panic attacks. His wife of 15 years demanded that he seek help or she was going to leave him. One night she woke up and stood in the doorway of his study watching him masturbate in front of the computer while he was watching a pornographic site. She confronted him and demanded that he stop.

His history of secret sexual activities started when he was in high school when his mother divorced his alcoholic father. He lived with his mother and found another father in his athletic coach. He was part of a group of boys who regularly went to the coach's house to watch pornographic videos. He never told his mother where he was and she just assumed it was regular after-school activities. These were wonderful times for him because he was one of the boys and they all shared in this special secretive society. Like other teenagers, they were risk takers and they knew this was a risky behavior.

Suddenly one day his coach was not there. The principal explained that the coach had become ill and needed to take a leave of absence. This was of little consolation to George and the other boys who felt abandoned. They dared not ask too many questions and they were afraid to talk to each other, because they knew what they had been doing was wrong. George thought it was his fault that he let the coach show him those videos.

All he had left was these exciting memories and no way to recapture them. He craved the excitement and nothing would give him any relief. He was irritable, depressed, and he never felt satisfied doing anything. For the first time he fell behind in his homework and his GPA dropped. His mother finally realized that something was very wrong with him and found him a therapist.

Neither he nor his therapist mentioned his sex life. He was too ashamed to bring it up and the therapist failed to ask about it. He spent many hours playing video games by himself. He would get lost in them, often feeling as if he was being drawn into the depths of the monitor. He had an occasional girlfriend, but never a sexual relationship.

George entered college to major in education and biology, but he changed his major when he discovered computer games in the computer lab and was instantly hooked. He felt comfortable with the people in the computer lab and learned about surfing the web from them. For the first time in years he felt part of a group again.

It was also in college that he met Mary and fell in love with her. They planned to get married after graduation, but she became pregnant. She would not get an abortion and insisted that he marry her. He was forced to drop out of college and get a full-time job. He still went to night school, but between the baby, working full-time, and his classes, he was only getting five hours of sleep per night.

One night after class, he fell asleep at the wheel while driving home and crashed into a telephone pole. As he sat in his car staring at the telephone pole he had a flashback of standing in the auditorium as the principal announced the fact that the coach was sick and not coming back. Shortly after the accident, he began having nightmares and early morning awakenings, and he could not go back to sleep again. All he could think about was that he had to find a way to the excitement he felt in high school.

The next thing he knew he was in an adult bookstore where he bought a CD for his computer. Even as he drove home with it his anticipation was almost overwhelming. He barely arrived home before he started to masturbate. From then on, he spent many of his waking hours secretly in his study. By this time in his life, George was married and had a baby. Sometimes he even brought the baby into his study when he was babysitting.

One night he entered a chat room and signed in as a single man looking for a single woman. He was immediately bombarded by Instant Messages (IMs). He was exhilarated by the attention he received and tried to keep up with all the people he was meeting. He quickly went from chatting online to masturbating while online. He continued to do this night after night until he would fall asleep online. He began to miss work because he overslept. He was afraid of being caught, so he alternated between chats to surfing web sites. His boss noticed his tardiness and absences and warned George that he would be fired if he kept it up. He stopped for a week. He was miserable, depressed, angry, and resentful of his wife who was enjoying their baby so much.

Finally, he could not stand it anymore and went back to his nightly forays looking for cybersex. It was shortly after that when his wife found him the first time. He promised to quit, which he did at home and promptly switched to another server at work. He told his wife that he had a special project at work and he would be coming home late. She did not trust him and called his office. She was told there was no such project. She confronted him and demanded he go for treatment or she would leave him. He agreed on the condition that she came with him.

METHODS

Inpatient Assessment

Initial assessments at the Program for Sexual and Trauma Recovery (PSTR) at Sierra Tucson include psychometric testing, psychiatric testing, history and physical, psychosocial history, and when warranted, HIV testing. Observational assessments are evaluated weekly at multidisciplinary team meetings, and treatment plans are reevaluated accordingly.

Additionally, in a preliminary study of 38 patients, the Beck Hopelessness Scale (BHS) (Beck, Weissman, Lester, & Trexler, 1974) was administered upon admission and upon discharge. The BHS was chosen as a pre-/post-treatment tool because many patients with some form of sexual addiction often report a sense of hopelessness, depression, and anxiety secondary to having been "found out" by spouses, family, employers, etc.

Outpatient Assessment

The following assessments were devised at the Computer Addiction Services at McLean Hospital in order to determine what kinds of treatment interventions are necessary to help patients who are entering this clinic. Table 1 illustrates the signs and symptoms of computer addiction (CA). The list was developed as a result of contact with clinic patients, numerous requests for referrals and consultations from other therapists, and many online requests for help. It is based on an impulse control model.

In order to make a proper diagnosis, the Orzack version of Anderson's internet addiction (Orzack, 1999) was administered. In this version the scale has been altered to include all kinds of computer activity rather than just the Internet. The scale was used diagnostically and not as a research tool. It was therefore possible to explore each of the questions in depth rather than just check off answers.

In addition, we found it advisable to add a new series of questions. These started out with the question, "What are your expectations when you turn on the computer? Are they positive or negative?" Such questions allowed people to make statements with more freedom than answering the scale. Welsh (1999) did content analyses of answers and found that those subjects classified as dependent had very different expectations from the nondependent subjects. The former turned to computers for relief from anxiety and tension, whereas the latter were neutral about the effect of the computer. Clinic guidelines require a treatment plan with a reevaluation of the patients' progress at three-month intervals. Each treatment plan is presented to the team and must be approved by each member. The patient is included in planning the treatment.

Inpatient Treatment

A useful analogy made by many experts in the field is that cybersex is like the crack cocaine of sexual addiction. Following that analogy, as a chemical dependency treatment model is commonly used to treat crack addiction, so a compulsive behavioral model such as a sexual addiction model can be used to treat a cybersex addiction. This is usually a mixture of cognitive behavioral therapy and peer support.

The highly structured and supportive environment of inpatient treatment (28–42 days) allows for an even richer mixture of modalities to change the addictive behaviors and thought processes. Cognitive behavioral therapy (CBT) supplies structure to disclosure and encourages proactive relapse prevention. Psychodynamic interventions (role plays, reconstructions, and gestalt) provide increased objectivity. Experiential-based therapies (team building and physically challenging activities such as climbing walls, ropes course, and equine therapy) increase trust and personal power and decrease shame. Expressive arts therapies (art therapy, movement therapy, body tracings) provide a stronger mind–body–spirit connection and address compartmentalized or dissociative conditions. Mutual support group experiences (12-step groups such as Sex Addicts Anonymous, Sex and Love Addicts Anonymous, Codependents of Sex Addicts Anonymous, Sexual Compulsives Anonymous, Sexaholics Anonymous) decrease alienation, increase working knowledge of daily coping tools, and increase realm of support as well as spiritual healing. Individual therapies such as Eye Movement Desensitization and Reprocessing (EMDR), acupuncture, and massage therapy support and balance the mind–body connection. Neurochemical processes are more stable with closely monitored psychopharmacology, if warranted, and a diet rich in natural foods, high in fiber, low in fat and sugar, and no caffeine. Family therapy provides an educated supportive environment for continued recovery.

Disclosing long-held secrets to and by family members is an integral part of family and couples therapy. A multimodal approach results in a faster process of self-discovery and self-disclosure than what can typically be offered in the outpatient setting. The process of disclosure is often prolonged by the need to drop defenses and trust others slowly. The constant exposure to the above modalities requires patients to begin to trust faster and show acceptance of peers in order to gain self-acceptance. The process unfolds with patients' disclosure to clinical staff and peers, then to partners and family members, and possibly later on to employers, depending on the situation. Irons (1991) cites disclosure of sexual misconduct to medical boards, for example, as a necessity for physicians' recovery. Schneider, Corley, and Irons (1999) conducted a study that underscores the concept of disclosure to partners as a process over time. Even though clients may say and even believe they have been totally honest, as insight increases, often new layers of self-discovery and honesty are possible.

A central treatment issue is the lack of ability to create and or maintain increasing emotional intimacy with a partner, family, and self. Online romantic relationships and sexual images can actually increase isolation from partners and family and further limit emotional intimacy in one's life. Though seeming very real, online relationships can satisfy one's fantasy life, making a real-life relationship pale by comparison (Ross, 1996). Depersonalization and objectification become a stronger theme as the addiction progresses while true intimacy and communication decrease.

Practical ways to allow more time for such personal interaction include limiting or abstaining from computer use. Some clients who must use the computer at work have arranged their offices so that the computer screen is in full sight of others. Another tactic is never to be in the office alone. Some clients have found it helpful for their spouses or other support persons to be the only ones who have access to a log-on password. Those who have home offices have set up strict "office hours" during which they have access to the office. However, all of these tactics can be foiled, especially by the cunning, baffling, and powerful addictive process. So, some have had to abstain from computer use altogether. After 90 days or more of abstinence, some have been able to use gradually the computer in a healthy way. Some have had to change their occupation or work position to be free from the cybersex addiction.

Outpatient Treatment

Computer addiction appears similar to eating disorders in as much as the most appropriate and effective treatment for each cannot have abstinence as the goal. One can choose not to gamble, smoke, or drink because the user's life will only be better as a result.

The majority of patients with CA cannot be expected to abstain from using the technology because most of them must use computers either in school or to earn a living. Treatment therefore concentrates on helping people to moderate inappropriate behavior rather than to eliminate it. Treating cybersexual addiction may be better managed by at least temporary abstinence from certain sites.

CBT is based on the premise that thoughts determine feelings. The patients are taught to recognize these thoughts so that they can identify the trigger points for inappropriate computer behavior. On a case-by-case basis, the therapist and patient determine what activities can be substituted for the inappropriate one. This has to be a collaborative plan and often involves attempting some small change in behavior for each session, such as scheduling time on a strict hour-by-hour basis with rewards that are material or self-soothing and nonaddictive. Often it may be as simple as taking a day off or buying a small gift for oneself.

Using an alarm clock or having someone else cue the patient can be quite helpful. CBT requires patients be given a fair number of assignments. Each session begins with an accounting of activities, starting with the positive accomplishments rather than all the excuses about why it did not get done. These assignments can also be motivating since most patients want to please their therapists. Many treatment programs using CBT include exposure and proscribing an activity. This is often used for obsessive compulsive disorder (OCD) and can be helpful in other problems as well.

On the other hand, Motivational Enhancement Therapy (MET) follows a less confrontational approach, and treatment styles can be more innovative. The main goal of this is to help people to want to change, hence the term motivational enhancement. It allows the patient and therapist to collaborate on the treatment plan and set attainable goals. The patient is informed from the very beginning that relapses are always possible and that they are not an indication of failure.

Even with this type of therapy the patient who is downloading pornography has to be motivated to want to change behavior. Empathy is one of the prime components of this therapy. Labeling is discouraged. Resistance on the part of the patient is considered a reaction to the therapist's style. Together they must solve this problem. A combination of both interventions seems to work best.

Since this is a very complex problem, patients are referred to a variety of auxiliary treatments including acupuncture, biofeedback, exercise, nutritionists, etc. The team on site includes family therapists, psychopharmacologists, and a case manager. Members are often called together or leave each other copies of treatment summaries.

Most of these patients are on a combination of seratonin reuptake inhibitors (SRIs) and nonaddictive, antianxiety drugs. Some even need an occasional antipsychotic medication. This combination helps concentration and thus results in more productive therapy.

RESULTS

Inpatient Results

After an average stay of 28 days, admission, and discharge BHS scores were compared. In the preliminary study of 38 patients, the average BHS admission score was 6.71 and the average score at discharge was 2.53. The average BHS improvement of 4.18 provides preliminary evidence that a multimodal, transdisciplinary approach to sexual addiction, in general, and to cybersex, in particular, can be effective in giving patients like Jeff both the tools and the hope that are essential to recovery.

Jeff has been successful in limiting his computer use to work, where he advised his supervisor of his addictive computer use. His supervisor and SAA 12-step group were supportive of Jeff limiting his work hours to those when others were present and rearranging his office so that his computer screen was more visible by others. He no longer works at home and leaves the home computer to his children and wife. This has also improved his work boundaries so that he has more time and attention for his relationship with his wife and children. As a result of her family participation, Jeff's wife was able to consider that she might benefit from seeing a therapist and attending the 12-step support group of COSA. This has helped her take the focus off Jeff's behavior, relieving her of the responsibility to monitor him and relieving Jeff of too much emphasis on pleasing his wife. With each focusing on their own issues, they are starting to feel more like equals and are rebuilding trust slowly.

Outpatient Results

George has responded to treatment by joining an SLAA group and learning how to avoid many pitfalls when he has to use his computer. It has been difficult for him. However, he not only entered individual therapy, he and his wife are now engaged in couples therapy. He contracted to stay off his computer except for school. It was a joint decision that he cut back on his job so that he could get more rest, attend SLAA meetings, and get much needed exercise. His anxiety and depression have been alleviated by a combination of Celexa and Neurontin. He still needs to use his computer for college, but, now that he has more time, he works in the computer lab instead of at home. If he has to work at home he does not shut the door anymore.

DISCUSSION

We have presented two cases: one from the inpatient unit and one from the outpatient service. As previously noted these were quite similar even though they came from different institutions. Each patient fits all the criteria for computer addiction, sexual addiction, and cybersexual addiction. Each patient, whether first treated in the hospital, followed up as an outpatient, or entirely treated as an outpatient, has been treated with a multifaceted program.

The major difference between the in- and outpatient treatments is intensity. When outpatient therapy does not result in the desired behavior changes, or is not changing behavior rapidly enough to keep the patient or others safe, inpatient treatment may be indicated. If SAA, SCA, SLAA, SA, or SRA 12-step group attendance is not enough peer support to reduce the denial or shame, or if a patient has too much shame to even begin attending these 12-step groups, inpatient treatment may be helpful.

As in all specialized inpatient programs, immersion and focusing on goals are an essential part of the program. The advantages of inpatient treatment with 24-hour staff and patient connection are obvious. Total immersion in a program that includes so many modalities is highly effective. A necessary part of the treatment often includes abstinence from television, newspapers, radios, and computers. Inpatient treatment without distractions also provides the individual with a respite from work and family.

Outpatient treatment, on the other hand, requires that the patient be motivated to make a commitment often for long periods of time. One of the major jobs of the therapist is to enhance the motivation using Motivational Enhancement Therapy (Miller & Rollnick, 1991). This commitment often involves family and friends who need to transport the patient for appointments. It is necessary for the outpatient to be motivated to recommit every time they come for an appointment. The CAS clinic even e-mails messages to patients at their favorite hour of midnight to reinforce their commitments. This may seem like an oxymoron, but phone calls do not work with these patients. Upon discharge some need continued outpatient treatment. Continuation in 12-step groups is encouraged, and many of the changes which Jeff and George agreed to should be continued. One problem with outpatient treatment is that support groups other than 12-step programs seem to be extremely difficult to arrange.

Although we have compared cybersex addiction treatment to an eating disorder model throughout this article, we in no way mean to imply that humans are dependent on computers for life sustenance. And, unlike human sexuality, computer usage is not an innate human need or drive. But, like television, telephone, and digital pager, it has become an essential feature of modern life.

CONCLUSIONS

Treatment modalities developed for treating other addictions, particularly food and sex addictions, are applicable to treating cybersex addiction. Inpatient and outpatient therapy programs can be modified to include cybersex addiction. Inpatient and outpatient treatments vary in intensity, but both include CBT, MET, problem solving, alternative therapies, and physical healing. Both include auxiliary treatment such as 12-step groups, peer support, family therapy, medication, and a continuous emphasis on relapse prevention. To conclude, cybersex addiction is an extremely potent addiction that must be treated as such. The extraordinary expansion of computer technology into more and more lives and into all parts of our lives means that cybersex addiction will increase.

REFERENCES

American Psychiatric Association. (1994). *Diagnostic and statistical manual of mental disorders* (4th ed.). Washington, DC: Author.

Beck, A. T., Weissman, A., Lester, D., & Trexlor, L. (1974). The measurement of pessimism: the hopelessness scale. *Journal of Consulting & Clinical Psychology, 42,* 86–865.

Cooper, A., Delmonico, D., & Burg, R. (2000). Cybersex users, abusers, and new compulsives: New findings & treatment strategies. *Sexual Addiction & Compulsivity, 7,* 5–29.

Goodman, A. (1998). Sexual addiction: The new frontier. *The Counselor, 16*(5), 17–26.

Irons, R. (1991). Sexually addicted professionals: Contractual provisions for re-entry. *American Journal of Psychiatry Neurology,* Spring, 1991.

Miller, W. R., & Rollnick, S. (1991). *Motivational interviewing preparing people to change addictive behavior.* New York: The Guilford Press.

Orzack, M. H. (1998, August). Computer addiction. What is it? *Special Report. Mental Health Computing. Psychiatric Times, XV*(8), 32.

Orzack, M. H. (1999). How to recognize and treat computer.com addictions. *Directions in Clinical and Counseling Psychology,* Lesson 2, 1999, Vol. 9, pp. 13–26. New York: The Hatherleigh Co.

Ross, C. (1996). A qualitative study of sexually addicted women. *Sexual Addiction & Compulsivity, 3,* 43–53.

Schneider, J., Corley, M., & Irons, R. (1999). Surviving disclosure of infidelity: Results of an international survey of 164 recovering sex addicts and partners. *Sexual Addiction & Compulsivity, 5,* 189–217.

Schneider, J. P. (1991). How to recognize the signs of sexual addiction: Asking the right questions may uncover serious problems. *Postgrad Med, 90*(6).

Shapira, N. A. (1998, May). *Problematic Internet use.* Paper presented at the annual meeting of the American Psychiatric Association, Toronto, Canada.

Welsh, L. M. (1999). *Internet use: An exploratory study of coping, style, locus of control and expectancies.* Unpublished Dissertation, Northeastern University.

Chapter 7

Compulsive Cybersex:
The New Tea Room

MARK F. SCHWARTZ and STEPHEN SOUTHERN

Masters & Johnson Clinic, St. Louis, Missouri, USA

Cybersex has become the new tea room for meeting anonymous partners and engaging in a fantasy world in which survivors of childhood abuse escape the demands of daily life as well as the pain and shame of past trauma. Compulsive cybersex was described as a survival mechanism involving dissociative reenactment and affect regulation. Descriptive data from a clinical population of cybersex abusers were reviewed to construct four subtypes of cybersex addiction. Treatment strategies for each of the subtypes were recommended.

Cybersex has become the new tea room for meeting anonymous partners for impersonal sex and enacting many of the rituals of bathhouse or public restroom sex. Compulsive cybersex represents a courtship disorder in which the "high" of being wanted by someone for sex regulates affect and bolsters a fragile self. The fantasy world of cybersex is a dissociative experience in which a person escapes the demands of daily life, as well as the pain and shame of past trauma.

Laud Humphreys (1970) completed an extraordinary research project focusing upon the behavior of individuals in public restrooms. He called public restrooms "sexual marketing places" or "tea rooms." Humphreys investigated the interesting phenomena associated with gay and straight (mostly married) men cruising public restrooms to engage in anonymous sexual outlet. The risk taking, game-like nature of the sexual interactions made the tea room trade more than a social encounter. The eye contacts and head nods of the tea room became an intricate dance of leading and following. The thrill of being wanted sexually by someone culminated in the addictive rush of ritualized sexual outlet.

Persons visiting parks, public restrooms, and other settings (e.g., sex clubs) for easy anonymous sex are captivated by the availability, invisibility, variety, and impersonality of the tea room culture. In Humphrey's (1970)

Address correspondence to Mark F. Schwartz, 16216 Baxter Road, Suite 399, Chesterfield, MO 63017, USA. E-mail: mfs96@aol.com research, restrooms in shopping centers located near freeways afforded ready access to busy men commuting from work. The 15 minute "pit stop" fit the fast-paced lifestyle of commuters just as well as fast food. Rapid turnover of prospective partners and introduction of many "one-timers" contributed to the allure of invisibility and the aphrodisiac of variety. Tea room sexual encounters were ideal for the married man with preexisting commitments to family and career because the impersonal relations were devoid of attachment and responsibility.

Cybersex has much in common with the tea room. Anonymous persons engage in easily accessible ritualized behavior that leads to impersonal, detached sexual outlet. In addition, there is endless variety of partners and sexual activities in this fantasy world. Intense orgasms from the minimal investment of a few keystrokes are powerfully reinforcing. However, compulsive cybersex users may find that more frequent contacts or more illicit activities are required to reach the original high of an idealized sexual encounter. In fact, compulsive cybersex participants frequently spend hours trying to locate fantasy partners or recreate role-play situations. Many of these compulsive users (i.e., cybersex abusers) are reenacting aspects of past losses, conflicts, or traumas in order to foster illusions of power and love.

CYBERSEX: WORLD OF ILLUSIONS

Once the senior author asked a woman whose husband had been jailed for incest how she remained involved with him when it was apparent that she did not like or love him and their relationship had no intimacy. She responded that she "needed someone to love her" or felt that she would die. This peculiar, irrational stance is central to much sex and love addiction. In cybersex, the desire to be wanted by another person is an essential element in the fantasy. Being desired is the thrill, the sex through masturbation is secondary. Depending upon the person's particular sexual schemata (Money, 1986), cybersex affords easy, inexpensive access to a myriad of ritualized encounters with idealized partners. One compulsive cybersex user seeks the perfect, flawless woman who will desire him, not reject him like the girls in high school. Another cybersex user wants the man of her dreams to "sweep her off her feet" just like the hero on the cover of romance novels. While some of the scenarios reflect dating motivations and romance themes, the encounters are illusory. The role-playing games are roadblocks to emotional and physical closeness. The remoteness of the computer keyboard (even the cybercam) interferes with genuine intimacy.

Cybersex fosters an illusion of power as well. The computer user perceives a high level of control through manipulation of the technology and the software. Nearly instantaneous responses to one's requests over thousands of miles of telephone cable contribute to the illusion of power and mastery. Immediate powerful reinforcement afforded by variable schedule "hits" make this behavior potentially addictive for many users. Cybersex participants can reveal as little personal information as needed to score with the right partner. Yet, this control of self-disclosure through role play and ritualized contact is inherently paradoxical when the underlying motive is being wanted or desired. In addition, the illusion of power is readily confronted by the image of the compulsive cybersex user spending hours at the keyboard, neglecting work or family, chasing the original high of seduction or allure as negative consequences are accumulating.

CYBERSEX AS DISSOCIATIVE REENACTMENT

Compulsive cybersex has some obvious and overt purposes, as well as covert and deeper functions. Obviously, the participant engages in the behavior because the sexual outlet feels good and there is a release of tension. There is at least an illusory connection to another human being to escape from boredom, loneliness, and emptiness. Heavy users of the Internet and compulsive cybersex participants are typically depressed (Cooper, Scherer, Boies, & Gordon, 1999).

The deeper functions of compulsive cybersex participation are not only illusory attempts to be wanted or desired, but also dissociative reenactments of past conflicts or traumas with underlying motives to resolve unfinished business. Dissociation means simply that two or more mental processes are not integrated. Dissociation is present when a person engages in secretive, illicit sex on the computer and then goes to bed with the spouse without dissonance or discomfort. When persons are overwhelmed by life experiences, dissociation facilitates alteration in consciousness in which aspects of self (i.e., behavior, affect, sensation, and knowledge) are disconnected (Braun, 1988). Some examples may make sense of the paradoxes constructed by dissociation.

A member of the clergy, professing celibacy and chastity, spends hours on the Internet cruising pornography web sites and masturbating while "cybering" with a teenage boy. He is a survivor of childhood sexual abuse, who is unaware of how he is reenacting the trauma in this distorted attempt to reclaim lost youth. A woman who had a pregnancy out of wedlock gave up her infant for adoption when she was 16 years old. At 35 years old, after having another child, she becomes addicted to cybersex contacts in which she is treated badly, like a "dirty slut." Her behavior reveals the unfinished contradiction in her life: "I may look normal and good, but secretly I'm bad and sexuality is the source of my badness."

Heterosexual men who had repetitive preadolescent sexual contacts with a male may become involved in same-sex chat and masturbation on the Internet as a means of reenacting the question, "Am I gay?" For some married persons, cybersex is an ideal mechanism for revenge or "payback." Compulsive cybersex users explained to their spouses when detected, "Somebody out there wants me if you don't" and "You spend so much money on what you want, I'm entitled to have my way." Some of the examples are so paradoxical they are easily viewed as perverse. An attorney in the midst of prosecuting sex offenders sits in his office and repeatedly masturbates while using his work computer. The father of three adolescent girls, whom he encourages to "just say no" to sex, retires to his study, and in a chat room solicits a teenager for a sexual liaison. The Dr. Jeckyl and Mr. Hyde quality of these transactions reflect the strength of dissociation in disconnecting parts of the self.

The survival strategy of dissociation evolved in childhood to manage disparate experiences such as tolerating physical abuse at home, while maintaining capacities for socializing and learning at school. Dissociation, through the mechanism of encapsulation, helps an individual forget overwhelming childhood experiences, which are fragmented and stored in various parts of memory. However, these dissociated experiences eventually leak into consciousness as reenactments. The woman who is unable to refuse any sexual advance and responds repeatedly to solicitations on the Internet cannot remember the incest from her childhood. Paradoxically, the compulsive reenactment through cybersex will not let her forget the abuse that is now repeated almost daily through the computer usage. In compulsive cybersex, it is likely that an ego state has evolved to reenact unfinished business, while the executive self-parents, goes to work, or otherwise maintains a normal lifestyle (Watkins & Watkins, 1988).

Cybersex can also function as a distraction from the burdensome consequences of selfhood, such as shame and perfectionism (cf. Baumeister, 1991). Any tension-reducing event, such as bingeing or purging in bulimia, self-cutting, or compulsively masturbating to orgasm serves the function of narrowing the perceptual field to concrete events and refocusing the attention away from distressing cognition and affect. Masturbation during cybersex suppresses awareness and expression of emotion.

The body symbolizes the playing field for working through unsolvable life problems. One cybersex addict embraced the numbing, depersonalizing quality of his compulsive sexual behavior. He had sex with his brother's wife over twenty years ago. His brother was killed in an accident two days after the affair. During therapy, he wondered if his brother committed suicide or, in a childlike ego state, he imagined he had caused his brother's death. He took his brother's place by being immersed in cybersex and becoming dead to the world. His cybersex ultimately became his dissociative effort at reconciling the unreconcilable: "My shameful, out-of-control sex killed my brother" and "I can't tell anyone, but my illicit behavior will eventually cause me to get the punishment I deserve."

Compulsive cybersex can become a primary or exclusive means of sexual outlet in which the survivor of childhood trauma encapsulates the overwhelming pain and shame of the past, reenacts salient features of the original events, and copes with the increasingly burdensome demands of selfhood in daily life. Compulsive cybersex users lead conflictual, fragmented lives in which there are many paradoxes. They attempt to escape from pain by harming themselves or others. Cybersex addicts want to be wanted but hide their identities behind false identities and ritualized role play. They seek closeness with detached persons who may be thousands of miles away. Compulsive cybersex users try to control alien and unwanted feelings by spending hours on the computer without regard for negative consequences, becoming utterly out of control in the process. They seek intense, immediate experiences through a medium that will insure depersonalization and objectification.

Eventually compulsive cybersex participants experience the "bottoming out" process in which powerlessness and unmanageability confront the illusions of the addictive lifestyle. They can become involved in a recovery process truly dedicated to finding lost parts of oneself by abstaining from compulsive reenactments and reconstructing the vulnerable self. In planning services for recovering persons, it may be useful to examine some characteristics of individuals who seek treatment for problematic cybersex use.

LESSONS FROM A CLINICAL POPULATION: CYBERSEX ABUSERS

Some preliminary descriptive data were gathered from 40 patients seeking treatment in an outpatient psychiatric clinic during 1995–1999 for problematic cybersex involvement. Half were referred by physicians or mental health care providers and half were self-referred, most of these participating in 12-step recovery groups for addiction (e.g., Alcoholics Anonymous) or attending community education programs regarding sexual trauma or addictive behavior. Patients in this clinical population were typically troubled by negative consequences (including marital discord, work performance decline, work rule violation, or shame) or excessive time involvement. Most members of the clinical population would fit the categories of "heavy use" (20 or more hours of Internet use weekly) and "pathological expression" discussed by Cooper, Scherer et al. (1999). Anecdotal and self-report data were secured from a chart review. While data from this sample of convenience should be interpreted cautiously, there were some interesting characteristics and interests among these problematic cybersex users or "cybersex abusers."

In Table 1, marital status and employment status characteristics reflected self-report data, while psychiatric status and addiction status were determined by doctoral-level clinicians. Most of the patients (57.5% of males and females) were married or living with a partner in a committed relationship. The largest group in terms of employment was white-collar professionals (47.5% of males and females), including several graduates of doctoral or professional programs. Another subpopulation of interest was composed of five single, female students (23.8% of the female patients). The demographic data indicated the clinical population was primarily college-educated students and professionals.

TABLE 1. Characteristics of Cybersex Abuse Patients

Characteristic	Male		Female		Total	
	N	Percent	N	Percent	N	Percent
Marital status						
Married/committed	11	57.9	12	57.2	23	57.5
Divorced	3	15.8	4	19.0	7	17.5
Separated	3	15.8	0	00.0	3	07.5
Single	2	10.5	5	23.8	7	17.5
	19	100.0	21	100.0	40	100.0
Employment status						
White collar	10	52.6	9	42.8	19	47.5
Blue collar	5	26.3	3	14.3	8	20.0
Homemaker	0	00.0	1	04.8	1	02.5
Student	2	10.5	5	23.8	7	17.5
Unemployed	1	05.3	1	04.8	2	05.0
Disabled	1	05.3	2	09.5	3	07.5
Psychiatric status[a]						
Sexual abuse	11	57.9	16	76.2	27	67.5
PTSD diagnosis	6	31.6	11	52.4	17	42.5
Affective disorder	13	68.4	16	76.2	29	72.5
Addiction status[a]						
Chemical dep.[b]	14	73.7	9	42.9	23	57.5
Eating disorder[c]	5	26.3	14	66.7	19	47.5
Sexual addiction	17	89.5	11	52.4	28	70.0

[a]Percentage based on total N, characteristics no mutually exclusive; [b]Includes 8 male alcoholics, 2 female alcoholics, 6 male drug addicts and 7 female drug addicts; 5 males in recovery for CD and 1 female in recovery; [c]Includes 3 male compulsive overeaters, 6 female compulsive overeaters, 2 male bulimics, and 8 female bulimics.

Psychiatric status and addiction status were determined by reviewing extensive documentation, including initial assessments, psychiatric evaluations, psychosocial histories, and other mental health assessments. There were 40 patients who were referred primarily or exclusively for problematic cybersex activity, typically involving masturbating or self-touching while communicating with someone on the Internet. The majority of patients presented affective disorder (72.5% of males and females) with only two patients diagnosed with bipolar affective disorder (5.0%). Over two thirds (67.5%) of patients had a history of sexual abuse, with females being more likely to present sexual abuse history and posttraumatic stress disorder (PTSD) diagnosis. There were inadequate anecdotal and self-report data to estimate extent of dissociative disorder in the population of cybersex abusers. However, patient descriptions of losing track of time and becoming immersed in fantasy were highly suggestive of significant dissociation.

In terms of addictive behavior, males were more likely to report chemical dependence (73.7% of males versus 42.9% of females) with more males in recovery for alcoholism and more females in active addiction to various drugs (such as benzodiazepines, narcotics, and cocaine). Two-thirds of the women (66.7%) reported an eating disorder, including compulsive overeating and bulimia (primarily purging subtype). Four of the five single female students would be considered obese and presented an eating disorder. One of the eating-disordered females was an African-American and one of the alcoholic males was Hispanic-American. The other patients (95.0%) were Caucasian-Americans. Therefore, this clinical population is not representative in terms of race or ethnicity.

Most of the male patients (89.5%) were self-diagnosed as "sex addicts" or would likely fit basic criteria for compulsive sexual behavior such as tolerance, drive, powerlessness, and unmanageability. Only half of the female patients (52.4%) engaged in compulsive sexual behavior, although their Internet usage and cybersex were considered by patients and/or their referral sources to be pathological.

Table 2 depicted the self-reported interests of cybersex abuse patients. One fourth of patients participated in cybersex associated with atypical or special sexual interests. Five males reported paraphiliac interests in sadomasochism, voyeurism, haircutting fetish, and zoophilia (sex with animals). Five females reported sexual interests in sadomasochism, exhibitionism, foot fetish, and biracial sex.

The next most common interest explored in Internet usage and cybersex involved romance and dating with males (21.0%) and females (23.8%) presenting similar levels of participation. Three males and three females used the Internet to become involved in the alternative lifestyle of swinging. Some of their cybersex activity constituted initial engagement in partner swapping or sharing. Overall, there were no major differences in interest according to biological sex or gender.

A few patients used the Internet to explore homosexual (10.0% of all patients) and bisexual (7.5%) preferences. Using the Internet to consider sexual alternatives has been advocated as a means for helpful sexual exploration by some authors (Cooper, 1998; Cooper, Scherer et al., 1999; Leiblum, 1997; Newman, 1997). Only two patients engaged frequently in "genderbending" or representing oneself as a member of the opposite sex,

TABLE 2. Self-Reported Interests of Cybersex Abuse Patients

Interest	Male		Female		Total	
	N	Percent	N	Percent	N	Percent
Paraphilia[a]	5	26.3	5	23.8	10	25.0
Romance/dating	4	21.0	5	23.8	9	22.5
Swinging	3	15.8	3	14.2	6	15.0
Chat/social outlet	2	10.5	2	09.5	4	10.0
Homosexual	2	10.5	2	09.5	4	10.0
Bisexual	1	05.2	2	09.5	3	07.5
Genderbending[b]	1	05.2	1	04.7	2	05.0
Teens/juveniles[c]	2	10.5	0	00.0	2	05.0
Total	19	100.0	21	100.0	40	100.0

[a]Includes S/M (2 males, 2 females), voyeurism, exhibitionism, haircutting fetish, foot fetish, biracial preference, zoophilia; [b]Presenting oneself as opposite biological sex; [c]Includes one male who engaged in cybersex with partner on teen chat line and one who engaged in cybersex secondary to role play on special interest chat line.

although pretending to be a different age or gender is not unusual in surveys of Internet use (Cooper, Scherer et al., 1999).

Two of the adult male patients reported frequent use of the Internet to explore their interests in adolescents. Both patients denied actual sexual outlet with juveniles, explaining that they used Internet pornography and cybersex to engage in fantasy relationships with teen school girls or cheer-leaders. Nevertheless, one of these individuals engaged in cybersex on a teen chat line, engaging in what could be considered predatory or "groom-ing" behavior. One of the female patients in the clinical population was a 17-year-old sexual abuse survivor who presented depression and compulsive overeating. She used the Internet to contact potential dating partners and, therefore, could be considered a complementary partner, vulnerable to the type of adult male patient seeking cybersex outlet with a teenager.

As depicted in Table 3, female cybersex abuse patients were younger (average age of 30.4 years) than male patients (mean age 38.1 years). Fifty-five percent of female patients were 17–36 years old. This age range approx-imated the age ranges of all female Internet users in an online survey sample (Cooper, Scherer et al., 1999) and their literature review. Most male patients (57.8%) were from the 37–46-year-old age range making them older than typical male Internet users (Cooper, Scherer et al., 1999). They were about the same age as the heavy Internet users (mean age 35.1 years) who were just as likely as the clinical population to be married (58.6%). All of the patients in the clinical sample presented distress and dissatisfaction with their behavior as reported by heavy users in the Cooper, Scherer et al. (1999) study.

Several generalizations from the preliminary descriptive data of 40 pa-tients seeking treatment for cybersex abuse may be useful for ongoing re-view (Table 4). These generalizations suggested that distressed, heavy users of the Internet who engage in cybersex are individuals who are suffering from the long-term consequences of sexual abuse. Cybersex abusers are survivors who have overcompensated through intellectual and professional accomplishments. This clinical population is depressed and dependent upon addictive behavior to cope with the demands of daily life.

The Internet presents easy immediate access to a wide range of atypical sexual interests, as well as anonymous, role-playing partners. The cybersex abuser inhabits a fantasy world in which the individual explores or reenacts

TABLE 3. Age Ranges in Cybersex Abuse Patients

Age range	Male		Female		Total	
	N	Percent	*N*	Percent	*N*	Percent
Ages 17–26	3	15.8	6	28.6	9	22.5
Ages 27–36	3	15.8	10	47.6	13	32.5
Ages 37–46	11	57.8	4	19.0	15	37.5
Ages 47–56	1	05.3	1	04.8	2	05.0
Ages 57–66	1	05.3	0	00.0	1	02.5
Total	19	100.0	21	100.0	40	100.0

TABLE 4. Generalizations from the Characteristics and Interests of Cybersex Abuse Patients

Cybersex abusers are	heavy users of the Internet
	generally married
	frequently college-educated professionals
	survivors of sexual abuse
	depressed
Male cybersex abusers are	middle aged
	generally older than female cybersex abusers
	similar to heavy users of the Internet
	more likely to be chemically dependent than female cybersex abusers
	more likely to be involved in recovery than female cybersex abusers
	more likely to engage in sexual compulsivity or be labeled a sex addict
Female cybersex abusers are	generally younger than male cybersex abusers and heavy users of the Internet
	similar to all (nonproblematic) users of the Internet
	more likely to present PTSD than male cybersex abusers
	generally involved in compulsive overeating or bulimia
	similar to male cybersex abusers in terms of interests in paraphilias, romance/dating, and swinging

traumatic abuse or overcomes temporarily the burden of psychiatric symptoms and addictive behavior developed to survive the pain and shame of the past.

Male compulsive users present cybersex as a manifestation of sexual addiction. Female cybersex abusers may be vulnerable to trauma reenactment as they explore sexual preferences and reach out to anonymous partners. Male and female cybersex abusers experience increasing negative consequences as they continue to participate in this high-tech form of intimacy dysfunction.

RECOVERY FROM COMPULSIVE CYBERSEX

The results from our clinical experience and review of the literature established that involvement in compulsive cybersex is not a unitary phenomenon. Compulsive cybersex is a complex, multifaceted experience that requires several levels of analysis prior to making recommendations for different components of treatment.

The medium of the Internet is essentially neutral or value-free. The burgeoning Internet and the technologies which reach out to foster a global information community are not the culprits in compulsive cybersex. In spite of the exponential increase in usage, the Internet contributes less than 1% of sexually explicit materials in the United States (Cate, 1996). There are features in the Internet, such as filters, which are more effective than print and broadcasting media in controlling access by children and vulnerable populations to sexually explicit content (Cate, 1996; Lamb, 1998). On the other hand, sexually oriented web sites and chat rooms are very popular on the Internet, visited daily by 9 million persons (15.8% of the 57 million Americans using the World Wide Web) (Cooper, Scherer et al., 1999).

Some clinicians have argued that easy, anonymous access to sexual content on the Internet actually facilitates sexual health through the exploration of sexual preferences and feelings (Cooper, 1998; Kim & Bailey, 1997; Leiblum, 1997; Newman, 1997). This group of professionals argued that the advent of the "information superhighway" offers new ways to discuss sex in a candid, nonjudgmental manner. They also found that "computer mediated relating" (Cooper, 1998; Cooper et al., 1999) established a foundation for expressing relational needs without the typical prerequisites of physical attractiveness or dating skills. Nevertheless, some proponents of the sexual exploration perspective warn that Internet sexual contacts may advance involvement in paraphilias (Kim & Bailey, 1997), lead to addiction (Leiblum, 1997), or contribute to harassment and abuse of women (McCormick & Leonard, 1996).

Other clinicians and researchers have emphasized the pathological potential of Internet sexuality (Lamb, 1998; Bingham & Piotrowski, 1996). Young's research on Internet addiction (discussed in Cooper, Scherer et al., 1999, pp. 155–156) indicated that some depressed, socially isolated individuals develop a psychological dependence on the Internet that is characterized by increasing time online, unpleasant feelings when offline, and denial of problematic behavior. Internet addicts, whom Young compared to pathological gamblers, tend to seek sexual and relational fulfillment through fantasy-oriented Internet encounters. Heavy users of the Internet (20 or more hours weekly), especially for sexual purposes, have many characteristics in common with male cybersex abusers in our clinical population.

Cooper, Putnam, Planchon, and Boies (1999) differentiated among types of Internet users on the continuum from sexual exploration to pathological expression. *Recreational users* engage in cybersex exploration to satisfy curiosity, but they readily become bored or indifferent. They are unlikely to progress to pathological levels of involvement. *At-risk users* do not have a history of sexual compulsivity; however, they may become vulnerable to developing sexual addiction after discovering the access, affordability, and anonymity provided by the Internet (cf. Cooper, 1998). At-risk users, similar to the cybersex abusers in the clinical population, consisted of two subtypes: depressive and stress reactive. The latter type included *sexual compulsives*, who suffer varying degrees of consequences from their pathological cybersex. This group is most similar to the male cybersex addicts in our study.

Male cybersex addicts probably present well-developed addictive personalities by which they not only escape the painful reality of childhood sexual abuse or other life trauma, but also the increasing demands of perfectionism and shame in their self-defeating, overcompensating professional lifestyles. They are depressed and engage in alcoholism and perhaps other addictive behavior that emphasize dissociation (e.g., pathological gambling). Their compulsive cybersex use may reflect one or more paraphilias or more generalized sexual addiction.

Female cybersex addicts may be referred for treatment earlier than the middle-aged male cybersex addicts, possibly because the sexual conduct is so far outside the limits of stereotypical feminine behavior. While their involvement in compulsive cybersex could satisfy the criteria for diagnosing sexual addiction, female cybersex abusers are more likely to have developed an eating disorder to regulate their affective state (cf. Schwartz & Gay, 1996). They are survivors of childhood sexual abuse who are experiencing PTSD and probably a myriad of other psychiatric and somatic symptoms. Their cybersex involvement constitutes significant trauma replay. Some of the women in the clinical population had been repeatedly victimized through interactions on the Internet and actually sexually abused through face-to-face interactions with men they met through computer-mediated relating. It is likely that female cybersex addicts are very dissociative. In addition to eating disorders, they may experience self-cutting, other self-injurious behavior, and distorted body image. If they are chemically dependent, their drugs of choice are probably anxiolytics or narcotics, prescribed by their family doctors to manage anxiety and pain, respectively. Some of the female cybersex addicts may be involved in swinging or sadomasochism initiated by their partners.

Some cybersex addicts probably develop problematic use because they are essentially loners who have become dependent on the Internet for contact with the outside world. Their initial or trial involvement in cybersex was likely an effort to overcome roadblocks to intimacy. However, the addictive nature of Internet sexual exploration did not assist them in making the transition from chatting online to socializing in person. Males and females in this group of cybersex addicts are single and socially isolated. Some females in the clinical population were obese by virtue of a long-standing eating disorder.

A subset of socially isolated cybersex addicts may be inclined to develop paraphilias. In this clinical group, cybersex allowed the person to operationalize sexual fantasies that would otherwise have self-extinguished if it were not for the reinforcement of immediate feedback provided by online interactions (Cooper, Scherer et al., 1999, p. 155). Some of these paraphiliacs may be inclined to develop sexual interests in juveniles if there are severe social skills deficits, dating anxiety, and emotional congruence with children or adolescents due to developmental arrest. Males in this subset may enter cybersex during their adolescence. They can be inundated with pornography (Freeman-Longo & Blanchard, 1998; Lamb, 1998), which fuels masturbatory conditioning and shifts these vulnerable young men toward avoidance of intimate partners.

The groups most likely to benefit from sexual exploration on the Internet may be homosexuals in the process of coming out, bisexual or "bi-curious" persons who wish to expand their pool of potential partners, and members of the transgender community (transsexuals and transvestites) who are seeking social support and resource access. Individuals from these groups may experience barriers to sexual self-responsibility in their communities. Therefore, Internet connections with others, including cybersex, may represent efforts to strengthen sexual identity, rather than pathological avoidance of intimacy.

Based upon our clinical experience and the extant literature, there are at least four subgroups of cybersex addicts (Table 5) who present some common and particular treatment needs. Two of the subgroups are based on gender, while the other subgroups reflect lifestyle limitations. The *loner* and *paraphiliac* subgroups, which include males and females, are not mutually exclusive, but they are clinically meaningful. *Male cybersex addicts* should become involved in sexual addiction treatment (cf. Carnes, 1991) including 12-step groups such as Sex Addicts Anonymous or Sex and Love Addicts Anonymous. If they were active in alcoholism or drug use, then primary treatment for chemical dependence is indicated.

Depression treatment and trauma reconstruction are central components in the treatment packages for all cybersex addicts. Depression is a core experience in all addictions. With the development of a sound spiritual growth

TABLE 5. Subtypes of Cybersex Addicts and Recommended Treatment

Subtype	Recommended Treatment
Male cybersex addicts	Chemical dependence treatment Sexual addiction recovery Depression treatment Trauma reconstruction Marital/couple therapy Sex therapy Bisexual/homosexual dissatisfaction therapy
Female cybersex addicts	Eating disorder treatment Sexual addiction recovery PTSD treatment Depression treatment Trauma reconstruction Marital/couple therapy Sex therapy
Loner cybersex addicts	Social skills training Depression treatment Trauma reconstruction Sex therapy
Paraphiliac cybersex addicts	Social skills training Depression treatment Trauma reconstruction Sexual arousal reconditioning

program in recovery, the depressive symptoms may remit. If there is a strong family history of affective disorder and the patient fits the dual diagnosis category, the person may be a good candidate for antidepressant medication and cognitive therapy. Serotonin reuptake inhibitors (e.g., Paxil or Luvox) are helpful for dealing with depression, anxiety, and compulsive symptoms. The goal of treating depression and related symptoms is to reduce the immediate risk of relapse in early addiction recovery.

Much of the chronic emptiness and dysthymia encountered in addiction may be attributed to the long-term consequences of unresolved trauma. Trauma reconstruction is the second central component of comprehensive cybersex addiction treatment. Schwartz and Galperin (1993) described in depth the trauma reconstruction and reprocessing psychotherapies. In general, trauma reconstruction involves abstinence from compulsive reenactment of sexual abuse, abreacting the trauma, and integrating split-off parts or ego states in an increasingly resilient core self.

Female cybersex addicts would likely require some primary treatment for an eating disorder, typically compulsive overeating or bulimia, purging subtype. The eating disorder reflects a distorted sense of self in which dissociation is used to modulate affect. While many members of this group would benefit from the spiritual growth process in Overeaters Anonymous, they will probably require some focal treatment for the eating disorder in order to tolerate trauma reconstruction. Schwartz and Gay (1996) described the treatment of eating disorders from the trauma reconstruction perspective. The clinician should be mindful of the comorbidity of self-injurious behavior, dissociation, and eating disorder. Therefore, manifestations such as self-cutting should be ruled out. In addition, the female cybersex addict may need assistance in dealing with intrusive anxiety and other PTSD symptoms. Fast-acting antianxiety drugs such as Xanax should be avoided since they are addictive and deprive the patient opportunities to learn in vivo coping techniques.

TREATMENT OF COURTSHIP DISORDER

Conceptualizing cybersex as principally a courtship disorder also suggests a number of obvious psychotherapeutic interventions: i.e., learning social skills, participating in rehearsals of dating, learning to self-disclose and express emotions, changing perceptions of self as attractive and competent are extremely useful. Typically, there are three components of social skills listed. Individuals in structured group therapy experience progress through levels of social competency at an individually tailored rate. First, the isolated cybersex addict is taught how to start conversations. Advice is given regarding dress and hygiene and how to maintain appropriate eye contact without distracting motor gestures; the individual learns appropriate self-disclosure, how to keep a conversation flowing, how to handle silences, how to listen attentively, and how to terminate conversations. The second step is for the man to learn how to ask a woman for a date and to make the date fun. Individuals who solicit partners need to understand the complicated sociosexual scripts of how the male and female typically initiate social interaction in our double-standard culture. A third step is to establish a moderate level of intimacy and self-disclosure with a consenting female partner.

Some individuals may be relatively competent in their social skills initially, but most have difficulty with moderate levels of intimacy. At this stage, single men and women are provided with suggestions regarding potential ways and means to meet partners. Once a partner is found, the men are given progressively specific, but flexibly graded, instructions such as a coffee date, going to the movies with a specific time to end the date, meeting in the partner's home with no physical interaction, then kissing and petting but no intercourse, and, finally, intercourse with a lot of nongenital touching. After each date, the client is asked to detail and evaluate his social experience and is then provided with specific suggestions regarding social, dating, intimacy, or sexual skills.

Another component of social skills is attitude change. Most cybersex patients manifest uneasiness with specific aspects of adult sexual functioning. Early in therapy, definitive sex education is provided, including the use of visual materials if indicated. As an integral part of this educative process, female sexuality is discussed in depth by a female therapist who simultaneously models the competent woman. Similar information is provided by the make about the male.

Cognitive restructuring is critical to successful rehabilitation. Therefore, destructive thinking styles require continual reassessment in all phases of the therapy process. Cognitions which are destructive to self-esteem include irrational beliefs, self-deprecatory preoccupation, negative self-statements, unrealistic expectations, anticipated failures, misinterpretation of feedback, and easily elicited defensiveness. Negative self-esteem is maintained by each individual's unique cognitive filtering system. During the therapeutic process, the cybersex patients' biases in processing input from the environment are confronted and explained by the therapist after which reality is tested by the client. Cybersex individuals are asked to attend to the positives rather than the negatives in their lives.

Another common problem for the cybersex patient is the feeling of being a victim of life circumstances, of constantly being pushed and pulled between undesirable alternatives. The socially immature addict will often respond to stress by moaning like a child, complaining, and blaming others for his problems. As previously noted, he evidences little capacity for self-responsibility or for taking positive action. Such individuals often display personalities that are unattractive to potential partners or tend to attach themselves to partners who will mother them but who may not be erotically stimulating. In response to even minor stresses, such as traffic jams, the cybersex patient may exhibit rage and then retreat into his fantasy world.

Instead of changing the situation or finding a constructive means of stress reduction, that is, taking the front door by confronting and managing the stressful situation, the man retreats through the back door into deviant sexual fantasy or behavior.

Yochelson and Samenow (1977) have documented errors of thinking common among paraphiliacs. Some of these errors are directly applicable to the cybersex addiction population also. First is the "closed channel." Rarely will the cybersex client tell the full story (at least initially) to the health care professional evaluating his problem. These individuals have ambivalent motivation. They despise their sexual acting out, yet fear the loss of these experiences since acting out is the one high that helps them escape their distasteful lives. Fabrication has been a way of life. Cybersex clients even lie successfully to themselves; for example, some cybersex clients looking at child pornography state convincingly that they are not aroused by children—until shown plethysmographic results of their erections in response to kids.

Total self-disclosure of the individual is requisite to successful therapy, much like the alcoholic who must begin his treatment program by admitting his problem. Clients deny the extent and seriousness of their behavior and minimize the effects on themselves and others. They minimize others' re-lated deviant behavior and also minimize traumatic details of their past, as well as the desperateness of their current lives. Lack of trust is also signifi-cant in this context. The cybersex client will not allow himself to even hope that change in his acting out behavior is possible until other group members talk about their control. A positive attitude is necessary for change and is initially established as the client talks with other group members and with the therapists.

Marital or couple therapy should be offered in treatment packages for male and female cybersex addicts. Since most cybersex addicts are married, involvement in the extramarital sexual outlet typically produces injuries like an affair. After dealing with the immediate crises and conflicts, it will be necessary to address the intimacy dysfunction or attachment disorder under-lying the marital discord or devitalization. Each partner presents their own unfinished business from the past and structural deficits of the self. In fact, the cybersex may be the means by which the troubled couple unconsciously colludes to maintain safe distance. Therefore, they will need substantial therapy to restructure their relationship and acquire the skills needed to sustain true intimacy. Marital therapy may be quite difficult in swinging couples, espe-cially when one partner wants to maintain this alternative lifestyle.

Sex therapy is an essential adjunct to marital therapy. The goal is to overcome dissociation and trauma replay by getting back to the body and the natural sexual function. Even when there is no specific sexual dysfunc-tion or dissatisfaction to address, sensate focus is a recommended tool for establishing and maintaining enhanced capacity for intimacy. Southern (1999) recently described sex therapy techniques for intimacy enhancement. Sex therapy is indicated for loner cybersex addicts because many of this subtype will need assistance in overcoming anxiety and establishing sexual arousal or orgasm. Many of the sex therapy exercises can be accomplished through self-touching, although eventually it will be desirable to recruit a safe, understanding partner for sensate focus and related activities.

Social skills training is indicated for loner and paraphiliac cybersex addicts. This training involves individual and group approaches designed to enhance communication, assertion, prosocial, and dating skills in vivo whenever possible. The skills training incorporates demonstration, modeling, coaching, live and videotaped practice, and transfer of learning to real-life situations. We have used occupational therapy interns and other allied health staff members to help socially isolated, anxious patients practice coping and social skills in restaurants, shopping malls, and movie theaters. Dance and movement therapists have assisted some patients in developing grace and body comfort.

Most paraphiliac cybersex addicts will need some intensive treatment to recondition sexual arousal. Penile plethysmography can be used to monitor changes in sexual arousal from variant to partner-oriented preferences. Masturbation homework exercises are prescribed to suppress paraphiliac arousal that interferes with intimate sexual functioning with a consenting adult partner. Sexual arousal reconditioning is a prerequisite for conjoint sex therapy, although it may be offered concurrently with social skills training. Although sexual arousal reconditioning is recommended specifically for treatment of paraphiliac cybersex addicts, all sex and relational therapies essentially countercondition anxiety and remove roadblocks to sexual health.

In the Masters and Johnson Relational Therapy model, cybersex addiction is treated as a courtship disorder. Sex is a natural function that facilitates and expresses intimacy in a committed relationship (Masters & Johnson, 1970, 1976). The couple is the "patient" or unit of treatment. Initial treatment ideally involves a 10–14-day period of isolation from daily home and work responsibilities. During this intensive phase of treatment, the recovering cybersex addict and partner devote themselves to "trying on" different ways of interacting.

Many cybersex addicts living in close quarters with a partner will evidence a myriad of resistances to intimacy. These resistances are diagnostic, with such roadblocks being interpreted and neutralized in ongoing therapy. Cybersex fantasies can be used to access and "decode" life trauma experiences, as well as determine the developmental level (Schwartz, 1992; Schwartz & Southern, 1999). Helping each partner understand their contributions to a single avoidant or destructive transaction prepares the couple for new styles of relating. Blocks to intimacy originating in the past are manifested in the present, then confronted and ameliorated in therapy. Many patients will be emotionally rigid and respond with childlike defenses. Frequently, their ambivalence about losing the mood-altering properties of the cybersex will produce self-sabotage. However, empathic encouragement and guided homework help the couple overcome their fear of success.

We believe it is possible to investigate, describe, understand, and treat the emergent problem of compulsive cybersex. If only 8% of the users of the Internet present cybersex abuse or addiction, this is still a staggering four and a half million persons (Cooper, Scherer et al., 1999). Although some clinicians and researchers emphasize the potential value of the Internet for sexual exploration, many depressed survivors of sexual abuse should be considered a population at risk for developing cybersex addiction. While additional regulation of the Internet is unnecessary or unlikely to inhibit variant sexuality (Cate, 1996; Lamb, 1998), we believe that risks of heavy Internet use should be included in contemporary sex education (Cooper, Scherer et al., 1999). There are at least four subtypes of cybersex addiction and several related patterns of cybersex abuse in the clinical population we studied. We have offered treatment components corresponding to the major subtypes. However, we recommend ongoing clinical research to refine our understanding of compulsive cybersex.

REFERENCES

Baumeister, R. F. (1991). *Escaping the self: Alcoholism, spirituality, masochism, and other flights from the burden of selfhood.* New York: Basic Books.

Bingham, J. E., & Piotrowski, C. (1996). Online sexual addiction: A contemporary enigma. *Psychological Reports, 79*(1), 257–258.

Braun, B. (1988). The BASK (behavior, affect, sensation, knowledge) model of dissociation. *Dissociation, 1,* 16–23.

Carnes, P. (1991). *Don't call it love: Recovery from sexual addiction.* New York: Bantam Books.

Cate, F. H. (1996). Cybersex: Regulating sexually explicit expression on the Internet. *Behavioral Sciences & the Law, 14*(2), 145–166.

Cooper, A. (1998). Sexuality and the Internet: Surfing into the new millennium. *Cyberpsychology & Behavior, 1,* 181–187.

Cooper, A., Putnam, D. E., Planchon, L. A., & Boies, S. C. (1999). Online sexual compulsivity: Getting tangled in the net. *Sexual Addiction & Compulsivity, 6*(2), 79–104.

Cooper, A., Scherer, C. R., Boies, S. C., & Gordon, B. L. (1999). Sexuality on the Internet: From sexual exploration to pathological expression. *Professional Psychology: Research and Practice, 30*(2), 154–164.

Freeman-Longo, R. E., & Blanchard, G. T. (1998). *Sexual abuse in America: Epidemic of the 21st century.* Brandon, VT: Safer Society Press.

Humphreys, L. (1970). *Tearoom trade: Impersonal sex in public places.* Chicago, IL: Aldine Publishing.

Kim, P. Y., & Bailey, J. M. (1997). Sidestreets on the information superhighway: Paraphilias and sexual variations on the Internet. *Journal of Sex Education & Therapy, 22*(1), 35–43.

Lamb, M. (1998). Cybersex: Research notes on the characteristics of the visitors to online chat rooms. *Deviant Behavior, 19*(2), 121–135.

Leiblum, S. (1997). Sex and the net: Clinical implications. *Journal of Sex Education & Therapy, 22*(1), 21–28.

McCormick, N., & Leonard, J. (1996). Gender and sexuality in the cyberspace frontier. *Women & Therapy, 19*(4), 109–119.

Masters, W. H., & Johnson, V. E. (1970). *Human sexual inadequacy.* New York: Bantam Books.

Masters, W. H., & Johnson, V. E. (1976). Principles of the new sex therapy. *American Journal of Psychiatry, 133*(5), 548–555.

Money, J. (1986). *Lovemaps.* New York: Irvington Publishers.

Newman, B. (1997). The use of online services to encourage exploration of ego-dystonic sexual interests. *Journal of Sex Education & Therapy, 22*(1), 45–48.

Schwartz, M. F. (1992). Sexual compulsivity as post-traumatic stress disorder: Treatment perspectives. *Psychiatric Annals, 22*(6), 333–338.

Schwartz, M. F., & Galperin, L. (1993). Dissociation and treatment of compulsive reenactment of trauma: Sexual compulsivity. In M. Hunter (Ed.), *The sexually abused male, Vol. 3.* Lexington, MA: Lexington Books.

Schwartz, M. F., & Gay, P. (1996). Physical and sexual abuse, neglect and eating disorder symptoms. In M. F. Schwartz & L. Cohn (Eds.), *Sexual abuse and eating disorders.* New York: Brunner/Mazel.

Schwartz, M. F., & Southern, S. (1999). Manifestations of damaged development of the human affectional systems and developmentally based psychotherapies. *Sexual Addiction & Compulsivity, 6*(3), 163–175.

Southern, S. (1999). Facilitating sexual health: An overview of intimacy enhancement techniques for sexual dysfunction. *Journal of Mental Health Counseling, 21*(1), 15–32.

Watkins, J. G., & Watkins, H. H. (1988). The management of malevolent ego states in multiple personality disorder. *Dissociation, 1,* 67–72.

Yochelson, S., & Samenow, S. (1977). *The criminal personality.* New York: Jason Aronson.

INDEX